To my own dear fions

— It's so wonderful to
find something that
could only have
come from me to you —

lots of love,

Tomy.
xxx.

EVERYONE MUST LEAVE

EVERYONE MUST LEAVE
THE DAY THEY STOPPED THE NATIONAL

Nigel Payne and Dominic Hart

MAINSTREAM
PUBLISHING

EDINBURGH AND LONDON

First published in Great Britain in 1998 by
MAINSTREAM PUBLISHING COMPANY (EDINBURGH) LTD
7 Albany Street
Edinburgh EH1 3UG

ISBN 1 84018 053 6

A catalogue record for this book is available from the British Library

Typeset in 12 on 14pt Sabon
Printed and bound in Great Britain by Butler & Tanner Ltd, Frome

Contents

Acknowledgements

The authors are very grateful to the following for all their help: the management and staff of Aintree Racecourse, in particular Joe McNally, Barbara McCarthy and Karan White; Dave Sherren for his hospitality and kindness during their many visits to Liverpool; the Merseyside Police press office; the *Liverpool Daily Post and Echo*, and everyone who they interviewed.

Nigel Payne would like to thank his son Tom and Jon Hill of Wallace & Associates of Chalfont St Giles for their computer skills and ability to recover what he thought he'd lost. He also thanks Dominic for putting up with him.

Dominic Hart would like to thank Rebekah, without whose support and friendship this book would never have been completed and to Nigel for doing the worrying.

The Grand National has been part of our heritage since the early 19th century. It is always a spectacular occasion which captures the imagination of racing and sporting enthusiasts throughout the world.

I was delighted to visit Aintree on Grand National Day in 1997 to unveil a bronze in honour of Sir Peter O'Sullevan, CBE to commemorate his 50th and last commentary.

The events that followed soon afterwards are the subject of this book and I would like to wish the authors every success. Many fascinating stories have unfolded and the outstanding kindness and hospitality of the people of Merseyside will be remembered for many years to come.

I was lucky enough to be able to return two days later for the first ever Monday National, and the atmosphere was extraordinary. We owe a debt of gratitude to all those who played their part in re-staging the Grand National.

Anne

1

The Magic of Aintree

IN 1839, on Tuesday 26 February, a horse called Lottery became the first winner of the Grand National. Nine years later, Mr E.W. Topham took over the lease of Aintree and at the same time became clerk of the course. The racecourse land was then owned by Lord Sefton and it was almost exactly 100 years later that the Topham family bought the course outright. Some may argue that a career in the theatre is not necessarily appropriate training for a role in running the world's greatest race. Funnily enough in the more forward thinking times that racing now finds itself and with the realisation that we are very much part of the entertainment business, were an actress of considerable repute to take over the reins today it might not seem so strange as it did in 1949. This was the year when Mrs Mirabel Topham, chairman of the Topham Company since 1937 was handed the task of continuing to bring Aintree into modern times.

There are three impressive courses at Aintree: the Grand National and the Hurdle courses and the Mildmay course developed by Mrs Topham, named after Lord Mildmay and opened in 1953. Nowadays such great races as the Mumm Melling Chase and the Martell Cup are run over this course and are highlights of the Thursday and Friday cards at the three-day meeting.

On the far side of the Melling Road you can still see the grand prix circuit, also developed by Mrs Topham. At the time of its opening soon after the Mildmay course it was reputed to be amongst the best in the world. There were no fewer than five

British Grands Prix staged at Aintree and it was here that Stirling Moss won his first Grand Prix in 1955 and in 1962 the late Jim Clark, rated by many to be the best of all time, was the victorious driver. Very often, when I pay one of my many visits to Aintree, I treat myself to a little bit of a race around the circuit dreaming as we all do of the glory of being an idolised Grand Prix superstar. What is now very obvious is that the track does not seem quick and is light years away from a present day Formula One circuit.

The first real fears for the future of Aintree loomed in 1965. The course had suffered some lean times and it was rumoured there were plans afoot to sell it for development. Ten years later it really did seem to have been the last in a long line of 'last' Grand Nationals. After the Topham era Liverpool property developer Bill Davies became owner of Aintree Racecourse and, as his business interests would suggest, he considered Aintree to be a large building site, not an historic racecourse, home of the world's greatest race. However by late 1975, it was clear that Mr Davies had backed a loser as without planning permission, which was never likely to be forthcoming, his plans were severely hampered to say the least. Mr Davies had run the previous two Nationals with his own team but with very little success. Not surprisingly, he had made it abundantly clear that he would not be running any more himself. In early December, only four months before the race, the rulers of the racing industry seemed to have accepted the inevitable and were considering switching the great race to Doncaster where all its identity would have been lost for ever.

The racing industry, the Levy Board and the Treasury, the three major players, all seemed prepared to let Aintree die but fortunately the chairman of Britain's most successful off-course bookmaking firm took a different outlook. Many people have taken a great deal of credit, most of it justifiable, for the part they have played in the protection and development of the Grand National and Aintree Racecourse. Sadly, in my view, not enough of this credit has been pointed in the direction of Cyril Stein of Ladbrokes. It was Cyril who, at the 11th hour, negotiated a seven-year tenancy deal with Bill Davies, whereby Ladbrokes, on payment of a significant fee, would take over the management of the site and consequently the race for this stated period.

On 28 December 1975 Ladbrokes found themselves with a run-down site, no previous experience in racecourse management and with the world's greatest race some three months away. Many still familiar names were called in to put the show on the road. These include two of racing's best and most forward-thinking entrepreneurs: John Hughes, who died in 1988, and Rod Fabricius, now the highly successful and well respected general manager of Goodwood. Also there were Mike Dillon, now the voice of Ladbrokes who, when he arrived at Aintree the day after Cyril had done the deal, had to scale the perimeter fence and set off in search of the keys, and Lynn Wall who now owns and runs RTA Publicity, one of the most successful signage and stadium dressing organisations in the UK. Lynn still works at Aintree every year.

At that time I was marketing manager of the betting shop division of Ladbrokes and was fortunate enough to be asked to join the team to head up the marketing and promotional effort. It is no coincidence that Rod, Lynn and Mike are still amongst my closest friends in racing and I am sure that John would be if he was still alive.

Ladbrokes ran the National for the next seven years and considering that they were not able to make any long term financial commitments there is no doubt that they made a more than adequate job of it. We certainly had some great times in this period, some of Aintree's greatest in fact. We witnessed Red Rum's history-making triumph in 1977 and his subsequent appearance with Ginger McCain on BBC's *Sports Review of the Year*. Then there was the Bob Champion and Aldaniti victory in 1981.Without wishing to seem melodramatic I can well remember weeping unashamedly on both occasions. This was the era of Emlyn Hughes' great Liverpool sides and just like many present day footballers they loved their racing. When they weren't playing, travelling or on a three line whip for training we saw a lot of them. Mike Dillon and I used to have our press office based in a small caravan right below Aintree's County Stand and on more than one occasion we enjoyed the company of the players with their crates of lager. I can clearly remember Terry McDermott, now number two at Newcastle United, settling down to answer our telephones with the response 'Aintree press office' in his broad scouser accent.

Mike Dillon became good friends with a lot of the players at Liverpool and as 1978 was Emlyn Hughes's testimonial year Mike suggested to Clerk of the Course John Hughes that we name a race in Emlyn's honour. John readily agreed and the last race on Thursday was renamed The Emlyn Hughes Handicap Hurdle. It was run over two miles five furlongs. Emlyn returned the favour and the whole team came to the races proudly parading the European Cup Winners' Cup. This was the first time the cup was seen in public with its new owners and was tremendous publicity for the meeting.

It was also in the '70s that Aintree made its first positive steps to attract Irish runners. Mike persuaded us to hold a press and trainers' lunch at the Gresham Hotel, Dublin. We went along with the plan and Mike invited 40 guests. Despite the fact that we got no replies to our invitations, Mike was still determined to go ahead so we travelled over with some trepidation. At one o'clock Mike was starting to look a shade edgy as we still had no guests. We should have had more faith as at quarter past one we had our first arrival straight from his yard, still wearing his green wellies! The final outcome was that after inviting 40, 48 turned up. We had a magnificent afternoon and the bond between Aintree and the Irish trainers was well and truly formed.

Mr Stein had made it very clear from the outset that once Ladbrokes' seven years was up that would be the end of their commitment but despite this as we approached the 1982 race there were cries from within racing that this could be the last Grand National. How could the powers that be let us reach that stage again? Ladbrokes had done their bit and it used to enrage me when the cynics claimed that the only reason Ladbrokes saved the National was because they made so much money out of the betting. The National attracts a far greater betting turnover than any other race by many, many times but in fact it has never been a particularly profitable race for the bookmakers because almost every horse is well backed, there is an enormous number of small each way bets, and the odds are always on the lengthy side.

Fortunately a few of racing's aficionados did seem to understand the seriousness of the situation and a 'Save the National' public appeal, spearheaded by Lord Vestey and Johnny Henderson, the then chairman of Racecourse Holdings Trust, was launched in an attempt to raise the funds to buy the course from Bill Davies. Bill Davies agreed to a year's grace and under a similar rental deal the 1983 National was run under the auspices of the Jockey Club. The appeal fell far short of the price being demanded by Mr Davies and he was in no mood to extend his generosity and who could blame him. It really did look as if we had reached the end of the line.

It was to the race's great fortune that Lord (John) Oaksey wrote an impassioned piece in *The Telegraph* which was read by life-long Aintree fanatic Ivan Straker, the then Chairman of Seagram in the UK. Ivan refused to accept that the race was dead, and called the president of Seagram Worldwide, Edgar Bronfman Jnr. That same day Seagram were able to finance a deal which enabled the racecourse to be acquired by the Jockey Club and run by their subsidiary Racecourse Holdings Trust and at the same time they agreed to sponsor the meeting. The Seagram Grand National was born and the race was run under this title for seven years.

In 1991 Seagram achieved the ultimate publicity coup when the race was won by a horse called Seagram. There was really no more they could achieve so in 1992 the sponsorship mantle was passed to Martell Cognac, a subsidiary of Seagram Distillers. Martell, as sponsors, have become the envy of the racing world and recently renewed their agreement with Aintree. It will be the Martell Grand National until at least the year 2004.

Being press officer for the National brings with it its own tales and I have often wished that I had written everything down, year after year, as there would be a fascinating book. The one thing you can be sure of with the National is the absolute certainty that a magical story will unfold; the media man's dream, it has often been said.

It's probably asking for trouble to record this but for many years I have dreamt of having a runner in the National and it has to be said that on two occasions my dream nearly came true. In 1992 my good friend Peter Scudamore found me a gelding for a very reasonable £6,000. It was the time of the earth summit in Brazil and, as the horse's dam was called Win Green Hill, our partnership agreed that Earth Summit would be a good name for the horse. Nigel Twiston-Davies trains him at his beautiful Naunton yard near Cheltenham. He has been the most wonderful horse to own and has given us no end of thrilling times, not to say a lot of prize money too. In 1994, as a six-year-old novice, he won the Scottish National by an easy 14 lengths and after winning the Peter Marsh Chase at Haydock in January 1995, he was installed as 10/1 co-favourite for the National. Sadly he developed minor tendon trouble and was forced to miss Aintree. He returned to the track for the 1995–96 season and was cruising in the lead in the Greenalls National trial at Haydock in February 1996 when he slipped on the flat and severely injured his ligaments. The vets at Haydock were superb and partly because of them he has been able to return to the track.

Earth Summit's target is the National and I just pray he makes it. If he does he will have a fighting chance as he is the perfect National type. It would be a fairytale and needless to say my dreams have often developed into screams as he pulls clear up Aintree's long run-in and a few minutes later my partners and I are joining Patrick Martell on the winners' rostrum to receive the Philip Blacker bronze and to relieve Patrick of a very large cheque. You've got to dream and enjoy these dreams because leading in a winner is the most wonderful feeling in the world. If it were to happen to me at Aintree I hope Charles Barnett (Aintree's Clerk of the Course and Managing Director) will understand that I will no longer be responsible for my actions. Joe McNally (Aintree's marketing manager) reminds me of the great quote from Noel La Mare who said: 'I have three ambitions in life; to marry a beautiful woman, to become a millionaire and to win a Grand National.' Noel owned Aintree's greatest ever, the three-times winner and twice second Red Rum and I guess what he said just about sums it up.

Getting back to the real world, as I mentioned earlier, I have worked alongside such fine operators as John Hughes, Rod

Fabricius and Mike Dillon, all of whom played such a vital role during those troubled times of the '70s and '80s. I was also privileged to have worked alongside John Parrett.

John Parrett's death in his mid-40s in 1992 was a particular tragedy. He was Chief Executive of Aintree and I became a very close friend of his. He was one of the best operators I have ever worked with and I have no doubt whatsoever that he was on the way to the very top of whatever he decided to put his mind to. Those of us lucky enough to have worked with him will never forget his creative thinking and absolute enthusiasm.

During my time at Aintree I have negotiated with a broad spectrum of race sponsors including *The Sun*, the *News of The World*, Colt Cars, and from 1984 Seagram Distillers and Martell Cognac and have lived through the many 'last Grand Nationals' that I have described. Now, I am glad to say, the great race is stronger than it ever was. The viewing figures achieved by the BBC are amazing, regularly reaching audiences well in excess of 12 million and worldwide the race is watched by more than 450 million viewers. Some 20 television and radio crews attend over the three days, determined to capture some of the Aintree magic and press men and women from all over the world are accredited. I believe that the Martell Grand National can be called one of the top ten world sporting events and although the part I may have played in this could only be classed as minimal I have nevertheless lived through it and have been part of the great experience.

Not that 1993 could be referred to as a great experience more an unmitigated disaster, for that was the year of the void race following two traumatic false starts, a truly awful day for British racing, British sport and the nation as a whole. What happened on that fateful day has been well documented and does not deserve repetition, suffice to say that many people felt that the inquiry left something to be desired. In my opinion, some were apportioned too much of the blame and others got off too lightly. However I still depend on the racing industry for a large part of my livelihood so discretion is the order of the day. Maybe another time if the occasion arises and if any purpose can be served.

* * * * *

The build-up to the 1997 National had been extremely smooth, our relationships with Martell and the BBC were as strong, if not stronger than ever, and by mid-January advance sales had beaten all records. There was every reason for the Aintree management to be relaxed and confident. Discussions with Merseyside police had been ongoing throughout the 12 months since the 1996 National and as always they had been totally thorough and professional. Security is a major issue at Aintree and will always continue to be so. The enormous police presence together with our own security operation may seem to some overpowering, if not over the top, but nothing could be further from the truth. The Merseyside police are a truly magnificent force and their sole objective is the welfare of the general public. I cannot emphasise enough just how professional and self-exacting they are, and it is in no small part thanks to them that the final outcome of the 1997 race proved such a glorious occasion.

Our publicity build-up always starts in November with a visit to the stable of the previous winner so this time we all descended on Terry Casey's Dorking yard, the home of the great winner Rough Quest. What a day, but even torrential rain and quagmire conditions failed to dampen the resolve of the hardy jump racing types. It was here that we announced record prize money for the Martell Grand National, by some way now the richest race in the jump racing calendar, together with some revised race conditions designed to increase the field size without the risk of losing the class and quality horses. Charles Barnett and I had been working on these modifications for many months; the response following the Casey stable visit delighted us. The scene was set for a successful promotional build up.

All our other events and promotions continued in the same vein, the announcement of the entries (well up on previous years), the publication of the handicap weights (with a highly popular revised formula) plus the many other promotions we stage all led us to believe that weather permitting, 1997 would be a great National.

One of my major roles is to provide the best possible facilities for the media, including television, radio and the press. This is made far more difficult by the fact that we have to rely almost entirely on temporary structures and all the added problems this tends to create. The demand for accreditation is staggering and it never ceases to amaze me just how totally disorganised certain sections of the non-racing media are. You would have thought that the Grand National would be an event that the media plan in advance. They probably do, but it is a great shame that they very often fail to contact us until the last minute. With a multitude of requests in the last two or three days I find it increasingly difficult to retain a high level of courtesy – this could be a sign of advancing years which brings with it its own level of irritability, but more likely frustration that people assume that their tardy application is the only thing you should be giving any attention to. Naturally it's all sorted out in the end and people end up with pretty much what they need. Perhaps if we said 'no' a few more times that might speed things up a little. At Aintree we employ Mark Popham's Racenews service and they are responsible for feeding stories to the media throughout the meeting. More of Mark later as he was yet another who played such a vital role from mid afternoon on Saturday.

Thursday and Friday had gone really well, with David Nicholson (always a great Aintree supporter) carrying all before him. Richard Dunwoody, too, was having his best ever National meeting and by the end of Friday was almost assured of winning the London Clubs Trophy for the top jockey at the meeting. Charles Barnett and his assistant clerk of the course Ian Renton had done a great job in producing some excellent jumping ground despite the desperate shortage of rain. Aintree's new watering system and the dedicated ground staff had really done their jobs well.

Dawn on Saturday heralds the traditional breakfast at Aintree where the National contenders complete their final work outs and the *Sporting Life*'s Geoff Lester interviews connections and racing pundits to glean as much last minute advice as they are prepared or able to offer. One notable absentee in 1997 was the then Shadow Foreign Secretary Robin Cook who, although at the races later on, clearly felt that his early morning priorities lay elsewhere!

By 8.30 everyone starts to disperse, jockeys probably straight to the sauna, trainers off to breakfast and then to meet up with their excited owners or if their owners have braved the early morning chill, maybe this is the chance to walk the course and plan strategy. Like every event of this type different people have their own separate routines which they observe religiously.

For us the day now begins in earnest and there is the chance to ensure that everything is in place. Thursday and Friday have given us all a chance to get in the mood but this day is different, it is the only one that really matters, our whole year's work crammed into a hectic 12 hours. Like others, I too have a set routine and I work rigidly to a timetable. Everything must be right, there must be no errors.

In 1997 we had a lot of extra activities to mark the 150th running which included a parade of nine previous National winners. This was the brainchild of my friend and colleague Joe McNally and it proved a superb spectacle, a great idea except for the poor old horses who got well and truly caught up in the fun and games which were to follow.

Added security pressures were brought to bear with the presence of Her Royal Highness The Princess Royal who supported us magnificently throughout. The Princess Royal's first formal task was to unveil the bust commissioned in honour of the great Peter O'Sullevan and this one was down to me. It went well, Peter commenting that he had been positioned looking away from the paddock for fear of frightening the horses! It was now 1.30, the first race was only 15 minutes away.

By this time the BBC were well into their build-up and the vast television audience was beginning to grow. For my part I had to be sure arrangements in the winners' enclosure were all spot on and well rehearsed. Our team met to finalise any last minute details with the BBC's floor manager Owen Thomas and then I carried out my final briefing with the police. We all knew what each other was doing and we set out to anticipate every possible eventuality, such as the need for the police horses to be on standby, particularly if there was an Irish winner. That's when you can expect the whole of Ireland to join you in Aintree's rather restricted winners' enclosure.

My nerves started to jangle as the first of the runners for the big race entered the parade ring, their attendants proudly wearing their smart new jackets presented by the ever generous Martell.

I remember thinking that if I hadn't got everything in place by now it was too late to worry about it, a thought that nevertheless failed to stop the anxieties. The royal party accompanied by racecourse Chairman Lord Daresbury would by now have reached the saddling boxes en route to the paddock. Not long to go now before the real action began.

While I was in the winners' enclosure, there had been two bomb threats and my mind immediately went back to what happened earlier in the week when the motorways had been closed. The person making the threats had a strong Irish accent. I saw Charles almost immediately, with apprehension written all over his face. We formed up in his office right away, where some pretty horrendous discussions were to follow.

2

The Aintree Team

LUNCH on Grand National day went extremely well for Aintree chairman Peter Daresbury even though John Prescott arrived late and insisted on sitting in the wrong seat. After lunch Peter escorted the royal party to the parade ring for the unveiling of the bust in honour of Sir Peter O'Sullevan and later on went to Peter's commentary position with the Princess Royal to listen to him calling race two.

'We then went to the saddling boxes and I remember thinking that everything seemed to be going so well, and it was a beautiful sunny day,' said Peter. 'Whilst the Princess was talking to David Nicholson I saw Charles coming towards me and from his face I immediately knew something was seriously wrong.'

Peter Daresbury had made previous arrangements that if there were any problems a car would be waiting at the rear of the weighing room and the Princess Royal would be taken to a local hotel to await further communication. 'I was relieved and delighted that this all worked extremely well and she left the racecourse almost immediately.

'As soon as I was aware that the race would not take place on Saturday I was able to contact the royal party so that the Princess Royal could return home. Later that evening I spoke to Captain Tim Laurence to see whether Her Royal Highness would be able to return on Monday if the race was indeed to be run then and by a stroke of luck she was able to re-schedule her programme.'

After the Princess Royal had left, Peter joined the rest of the management team in Charles's office. 'During that time I became increasingly concerned about the plight of our customers and our inability to communicate successfully with them,' he said. 'People who were unfamiliar with the surroundings did not know were to go and families with young children were being split up. In hindsight, maybe all such events should have pre-arranged meeting places where people who have been separated could meet up.' Peter Daresbury also detected that overall control and key decision-making had moved away from the racecourse and as a result it was now crucial that Aintree representatives were present when these decisions were being made. Very shortly Peter and Charles were on their way to police headquarters.

Charles Barnett joined Aintree from Haydock Park shortly after John Parrett's death and was therefore christened at the fateful 1993 void race, the second year of Martell's sponsorship. Charles is a remarkable individual, often so outwardly laid back that it is unbelievable. I say outwardly because I feel that deep down the nerves will be jangling and the butterflies churning as with the rest of us but being the man in charge, Charles is determined that to the outside world he is seen to be relaxed and unruffled. I hardly left his side for the two and a half days that followed and I was full of admiration for the immense courage he showed.

Every year, about a month before the meeting, John Sunnucks and Kevin Byram of Brunswick PR put both of us through a rigorous day of media training, and the value of this investment was never more justified than it was during this period. We both had countless TV and radio interviews to handle and watching Charles, it was very clear to see the technique that we had been so painstakingly taught. He handled each and every interview with great authority and passion and if I had done half as well I would be more than satisfied.

Charles has a fairly small, yet dedicated, administrative staff working for him at the racecourse together with an experienced groundstaff under the management of Terry Robinson, who also came from Haydock. They all do a magnificent job and I for one am proud to work alongside them for so long each year. To add weight to the team at the National meeting Charles calls on the experience of Ian Renton, who acts as Assistant Clerk of the Course, and Richard Thomas from Haydock and Julian Thick from Kempton, both of whom are totally invaluable with their first-hand knowledge of the meeting. There are many others who join the team for the three days and Charles freely admits that, without this support, we would never have completed the tasks which enabled us to run the race on the Monday.

Charles was convinced that there was never any long term plan to disrupt the Martell Grand National. 'It was most probably a spur of the moment thing,' he said. 'The effect of Thursday's bombs on the M6 were probably the encouragement that was needed. When you think about it, it's all so easy; all it needs is a coded phone call and with the political climate as it then was, the effect was bound to be dramatic.'

Charles wrote down the timings of the two telephone calls on his trusty pad. 'They were timed at 2.49 and 2.52, as the horses were at the post for the Martell Aintree Hurdle. I just could not believe it and straight away I knew the consequences if the police were taking the calls seriously. I stayed on an open line to Ken Laidler in the police control room and he agreed that after the 2.55 race I should go straight to my office having called together all key individuals. I rushed to the unsaddling boxes where Lord Daresbury was meeting trainers with the Princess Royal. I bumped into David Hillyard (MD of Aintree's parent company) and he got hold of Judith Menier (of Martell) who joined us after warning senior Martell management of the alert.'

The route back to his office was a fairly short one but so desperate was Charles to get there that he barely noticed the confusion around him as racegoers began to fill the concourse, slowing down his journey. Soon after reaching the office, the alarms were activated, all TV monitors switched to *Operation Aintree* and all security staff put on full alert. The evacuation was already well under way. 'We stayed in my office for quite some time,' says Charles, 'We were unable to follow the progress of the evacuation as temporary trade stands blocked out the view from my windows. I remember glancing anxiously at my watch on several occasions as the first hour ticked by. It must have been about 3.45 that my police shadow knocked vigorously on the office door insisting we abandon the stands – if there was a bomb it could well detonate within the next ten minutes. We were to reconvene in police control situated in the horsebox park some 200 to 300 yards away. We all moved as quickly as we could.'

This was one of the most critical moments of the evacuation as the police and security staff were anxiously urging the thousands of racegoers who had evacuated from the main grandstands to pass through the central enclosure and leave the racecourse altogether. If there was a device in a vehicle it was essential that car parks were cleared. Running rail lay strewn across the turf having been torn down to make wider exits and the mounted police were shepherding people as firmly as they dared. It was essential that there was no panic, no stampede. For whatever reason there wasn't and for this the police must take great credit. It is most probable that racegoers still thought they would soon be back in the stands and that there really wasn't any danger. No-one really believed there was a bomb at Aintree.

After arriving at police control some fairly dramatic conversations took place, probably the most significant of which was confirmation by the police that racing would be abandoned for the day. The telephone calls had not identified any location of a device – it could literally be anywhere and, quite rightly, the police were taking no risks whatsoever. Charles adds: 'Desmond Lynam was conducting interviews adjacent to the main scanner and I went there immediately to pass on the very latest information to the millions of TV viewers, none of whom was sure what would happen next. This I did, and having told Desmond the seriousness of the situation I told him that everyone had to leave and leave now, and that included the BBC! Desmond has told me since that no-one had ever said that to him before.' The scene in this area was quite extraordinary, racecourse officials, trainers, jockeys, stable staff, TV and radio crews, contractors and seemingly hundreds of others. They all had to leave the course and make their way out on to the Melling Road, some, as it transpired, into the welcoming homes of warm-hearted residents.

Soon after his interview, Charles, together with Peter Daresbury, was driven in rather dramatic fashion to police headquarters at Canning Place where they were shortly joined by Judy Menier and myself. Charles recalls that journey with a mixture of amusement and anxiety. It was, he explains, 'totally hair-raising!'

Ian Renton is Clerk of the Course at both Salisbury and Wincanton in addition to being Assistant Clerk at Aintree. He knew there was a problem during the Martell Aintree Hurdle when Charles Barnett, who was with him at the time, was asked to go to a land line telephone. Ian went straight to the saddling boxes to ask the trainers and lads to take their horses back to the stables, then to the changing rooms via the weighing room to tell the jockeys and valets to leave. He stayed in the weighing room area with Bob Cox (who runs the public address system) to help sort out what may be required by way of public address when they too were forced to leave the area. 'When Charles left for police HQ my first major task was to evacuate the stables of all trainers, lads and stable staff,' says Ian. 'Only the horses could remain.'

However, it soon became clear that before long, evacuating the horses would be a priority too. 'Derek Thompson, our stable manager, had refused to leave, as had his son-in-law, who was down in the bottom yard where, amongst others, Jenny Pitman's horses were stabled. Charlie Brooks' staff, Phil Sharp and Simon Molloy had also stayed with race favourite Suny Bay.' Along with Charles Dodd, who runs the stable staff hostel, this group checked over and watered the horses and where required removed gaiters. Soon after 6 p.m., Ian Renton was given the go ahead for the mass horsebox exodus. Ian was particularly pleased to hear that the RSPCA had been quick to praise the efficient evacuation of the horses. Bernard Donigan, this organisation's equine consultant said: 'I would like to congratulate the Aintree authorities for their excellent organisation in getting the horses away from the racecourse and out of danger. Their actions indicated beyond any doubt that the horses' welfare was of paramount importance.'

'The majority of horses left either for home or Haydock,' explained Ian. 'I then remember being grabbed by Sue Barker to do an interview for the BBC which, courtesy of her employers, was washed down with a large Scotch. Feeling a lot warmer inside, I established contact with the British Horseracing Board's representatives who had gathered at the railway entrance on the Ormskirk Road. I was able to brief them the best I could including our initial thoughts about staging the National on a Monday. Later on the police agreed to escort Gail Brown, a freelance racing PR consultant, and me to the saddling boxes so that we could move all the gear from there to the weighing room where it could be locked up safely.'

Ian spent Saturday night at Peter Daresbury's house. 'It was a touch crowded that night so Charles and I shared a room. We didn't get much sleep. I woke Charles at 4 a.m. and we discussed the next 48 hours and what might be in store for us. In terms of Monday we would definitely run one race only, we would let everyone in free and we would lay on other entertainment. We were determined that Monday, too, should be a special day.'

This was Andrew Tulloch's third National and his experiences and memories will stay with him for ever: 'I will never ever forget Saturday night and my journey round the course to secure all areas and make the site safe.' Andrew was the first Aintree employee to get back on the racecourse after the evacuation and, as operations manager, and in the absence of his boss, took the responsibility of putting together a task force to tour the facilities to switch off gas fires, ensure the safety of all personal belongings, check all alarms, and, with caterers Letheby and Christopher, turn off potentially dangerous water boilers and gather together any remaining cash including catering takings that may not have been collected up by L&C's staff. Everything removed would be stored overnight and accounted for in the morning. He recalls: 'There was so much to do, and so little time to do it, as the police wanted us back off site almost before we had started. It was fortunate that we caught sight of two unauthorised individuals on our security cameras as this helped me convince them that whilst we would be as quick as we could we really had to do this job thoroughly.'

Apart from Ronnie Phillips of Lethebys, Andrew was accompanied by a police inspector, Major Chris Snaith from bomb disposal, who had rushed to Aintree from Catterick, and George Cowley, who heads up the internal security operation at the course. He also contacted the marquee contractors,

Championship Structures, to obtain keys to lock all the doors of the temporary facilities.

'We had to break into our main admission Portakabins to remove takings,' recalls Andrew. 'We carried out cash tills from around the site and we bagged up loose cash from Tote kiosks. This coinage seemed to weigh a ton and we needed somewhere safe to keep it. We decided to call up Bill Wilde of Special Events Parking and he agreed to store the cash in his caravan which would be closely guarded in the Steeplechase Enclosure. When Bill took his van in for its next service he was told he needed some essential repairs, the weight of the coins had apparently fractured the floor!

'We also moved all the valuable race trophies from the trophy tent back to our main offices and, whilst there, we collected such vital things as telephone directories and spare mobile phone and radio batteries. It was a sort of dawn raid on your own office.'

When his team arrived at the railway entrance, which is one of the main admission points on the Ormskirk Road, the place was in total darkness. 'Is anyone there?' Andrew called out. To his absolute amazement a voice replied 'About time too'. There, hidden behind one of the counters, was a member of the gate staff who had been sitting on his cash takings, probably for some six or seven hours. He proceeded to pass over two or three ammunition boxes full of cash followed by bag upon bag of the same. Andrew radioed down to Terry Robinson who drove up from his cottage in his four wheel drive vehicle and the money was loaded for Terry to take away and secure overnight.

When they visited the press marquee and press room it was a very strange sight. Laptops open and still powered up, fax machines buzzing away, and even the odd mobile phone ringing where it had been left. There were form books open already for post race analysis; it was as though an outside force had lifted everyone away.

Another vital task on Saturday night was to fuel up all the many on-site generators and eventually Andrew was able to arrange for a tanker from Preston which after some degree of negotiation was allowed access by the police.

'One of the most valuable items that I was able to grab hold of from my raid on the offices was my bible of telephone numbers and having this proved a real life saver. We desperately needed some extra landlines and had absolutely no joy in contacting BT. Fortunately our on-site engineers John Williams and Kevin Cunningham appeared when we most wanted them and worked feverishly to instal some lines. This enabled me to keep in regular touch with our various contractors, in particular the caterers, cleaners, marquee suppliers, the Tote and Racetech.'

Meanwhile another Aintree staff member was doing her bit out on the Ormskirk Road. Simone Roche, the course's conference and banqueting executive, is an attractive scouser with an engaging personality. What was happening in her beloved Merseyside was making her blood boil. Simone had left her bag and all her keys in the press centre and eventually she ended up sleeping on a friend's floor, having arrived there after midnight. She had heard that Radio Merseyside was broadcasting telephone numbers of places to stay so she rushed down to a packed Aintree station and arranged for public address announcements to be given out with the details. She then grabbed some cardboard boxes and marker pens and made some notices which she placed around the area. Her first port of call was the Sefton Arms immediately alongside the course, but in view of its closeness to the potential danger, it too had been forced to evacuate. The Queen's Arms was in full swing though, and Simone tells me everyone there was having a great time. She placed some posters in the pub and also placed her upturned boxes in the nearby petrol station, and on various lampposts and in telephone kiosks. She had not finished yet, and having somehow talked her way back onto the racecourse she helped sort out some confusion amongst some high ranking Specials who were reluctant to allow a shift change for Derbyshire Security, Aintree's own 24-hour operation. Eventually the change took place allowing certain members of the crew to get home following their 15 to 16 hour shift. It was after 11 p.m. when Simone finally called it a day and set off for her none too comfortable night on the floor. She had certainly done her bit for Aintree and Merseyside.

Richard Thomas left Aintree in 1991 and is now general manager at Haydock Park. Having had experience of three

Nationals, his first hand knowledge is invaluable when he returns to Aintree each year to assist in the running of the meeting. One of his roles in 1997 was to supervise the photographers at The Chair and the last Mildmay fence, both of which are situated in front of the grandstands. This is a critical task as the positions permitted have to be rigidly adhered to in order not to endanger any of the runners or riders or indeed the photographers themselves. It was from this position that he saw the activity in the stands as the evacuation commenced. 'Although we knew nothing formally it was immediately clear that we had to move racegoers into the centre of the course,' he said. 'Everyone was getting squashed so we decided to pull down the running rail to take the pressure off.'

Richard then worked hand-in-glove with the police and security firms to move everyone through the central enclosure and out of the course. 'People were clambering all over the fences so I positioned a man on every one. I knew that to have any chance of running the race it was critical that we protected those famous fences.'

Hearing that many of the National runners were to be taken down the road to Haydock, Richard's head groundsman, Maurice Crooks, was flown across in Martin Pipe's helicopter to prepare the stables. Richard decided that he too would head for home and at 9 p.m. he got hold of Charles, who asked him to come to Peter's house with Maurice Crooks at 6 a.m. the following morning. 'One small demand Charles made of me was to lay my hands on 300 to 400 security guards to be on parade at Aintree as early as possible on Sunday morning.'

Julian Thick managed to leave the course that evening in his own car. Julian is in the fast lane heading for the top of his profession. Now racecourse manager at Kempton Park, he is another with first hand operational experience at the National. His duties on Saturday were to control all car, coach and racegoer movement in the Steeplechase Enclosure on the far side of the Melling Road, working alongside one of the Bronze commanders, Inspector Bob Smith. 'It was Bob who alerted me to the problem, although at first we had no idea that it was anything more than an evacuation of the grandstands,' Julian explained. 'Evacuating the Steeplechase Enclosure had never really been considered an option and in fact, when the evacuation started, we had only just completed the task of clearing the inside of the course and ensuring that all racegoers were in their enclosures. Watching from the Canal Turn, I was amazed how quickly the stands cleared and both Bob and I reckoned that after a delay of say an hour, the stands would re-fill and the race run.'

A radio conversation with Charles Barnett soon dispelled this optimism, and it was confirmed that the whole course had to be emptied of people immediately. 'At first it was almost impossible to get people moving and one of our main problems was the inability to let people know what was going on. In the middle of the course there are no public address speakers, why should we need them, when, under normal circumstances there are no people there?'

Several cars had tried to make a run for it but the police stopped them leaving. 'About six vehicles actually reached the gate,' recalls Julian. 'You would not believe it, but the driver of the very first car was the owner of the fish and chip shop in my home town of Hereford.'

Julian stayed with Bob Smith for what seemed an age and when, later on, he decided to leave, Bob agreed to have his car, which was parked nearby in the Steeplechase Enclosure, searched and security cleared. 'As I went to start it up, Bob filled me with confidence by asking me to wait whilst he drove himself and his Land Rover 50 yards away!'

It was Aintree grounds manager Terry Robinson's first National and he well remembers his anger as damage was being caused to the fences, which had taken five weeks to build. Fortunately, in a spontaneous reaction, security staff cordoned off key fences such as Becher's and the Canal Turn which, as a consequence, were relatively undamaged. 'My problem was that it was not until after 12 noon on Sunday that I was able to walk the course and survey the damage,' he said. 'By this time we were committed to running the race on Monday, but no one had really thought about damage to the track and whether repairs could be made in the time.'

As it turned out things were not nearly as bad as Terry had at first feared, and as he accompanied the search team, ground staff followed about 200 metres behind repairing any damage and clearing away the debris.

'There were about 40 staff in all, including Haydock ground staff and our own permanent and casual workforce. The response had been tremendous, everyone just turned up determined to do all they could. Staggeringly as it turned out, the course was back and the fences repaired by 4 p.m. The whole exercise had only taken two hours, and both Peter Daresbury and Ian Renton were amazed what fantastic condition the course was in when they were able to walk it shortly afterwards.'

During the search of the fences a suspicious bag had been discovered alongside The Chair. The bomb squad produced their radio controlled 'hedgehog' which prodded the bag and they decided to destroy it with a controlled explosion. The bomb squad then approached the remains with caution only to discover the side of a packet on which was printed 'You've been Tangoed'. The bag belonged to one of the casual staff and it contained a large carton of Tango drinks. 'He was pretty miffed,' chuckled Terry. 'But he laughs about it now. Strangely, after this amusing incident the whole atmosphere became more relaxed.'

Armed with his list of telephone numbers on Sunday morning, Andrew Tulloch set about maintaining regular contact with his contractors so that their eventual return to the course could be planned. Senior management from caterers Letheby and Christopher were allowed access later on to assess the extent of the clearing-up operation and also to see what level of service, if any, would be possible the following day. Considering the high level of mayhem that they discovered it was remarkable that any catering outlets were open on Monday afternoon and that anyone was able to eat or drink anything.

Andrew particularly remembers a 6.15 meeting with Charles Barnett, Julian and Richard as being of vital importance. 'It was at this meeting that we set out our full operational plan to Charles,' he said. 'We agreed how we would ensure the site remained secure, how we would deal with all personal belongings, the creation of a holding area in the Horsebox Park and how we would combine our security operation with the police to search all personnel and vehicles on Monday.' It was at this meeting that Charles Barnett insisted that Andrew leave the site on Sunday night and return to Peter Daresbury's to get some sleep. Richard Thomas and Julian Thick were quite happy to stay and in the final analysis they worked through the night declining any opportunity there might have been for an hour or two's rest.

For Ian Renton one of his most immediate concerns on Sunday morning was the restoration of the racecourse and it was thanks to him that Terry Robinson got on to the track when he did, even if it did seem too late to the grounds manager. 'As time passed my fears were growing,' said Ian. 'It was during a conversation with Mark Sutcliffe, the head of the police search team, that I nearly lost my cool. Police communications did not appear to have been passed down the line, as Mark told me that the track should be clear by 3 p.m. This was bad enough, then he added, almost in passing, "tomorrow". It was then that he admitted that he was unaware that his senior officers and Aintree had just announced to the media that at 5 p.m. tomorrow the Martell Grand National would be run.

'I immediately formed up with Superintendent Ian Latimer and Chief Inspector Sue Wolfenden on site who, after a brief discussion, agreed that work on the course could commence almost immediately. Mark and I got on really well after this initial disagreement and I do fully understand the awful position he was in. As he pointed out, sometime in the near future he would have to satisfy his Chief Constable that the whole of Aintree's 250-plus acres were sterile, that there was no longer a bomb threat, that the public could be admitted and that the Martell Grand National could be run with total confidence.'

After leaving on Saturday afternoon for police HQ, the next time Charles Barnett was to see the racecourse was midday on Sunday. 'I was able to keep in touch but naturally I felt I should have been on site during Saturday night and the early part of Sunday,' he said. 'Thank God I had the team that I did. I knew that Ian Renton and Terry Robinson would be concentrating on the course and the horses and their connections and that Andrew Tulloch would take enormous comfort from the presence of Richard Thomas and Julian Thick, both of whom are first class operators and most importantly have a detailed knowledge of the site.'

Charles had decided very early on that he would, wherever possible, support the decisions that his team were to make. He knew that they would keep in close contact with Silver Command on site but being away from the course was not exactly ideal as far as he was concerned. 'Needless to say I was not let down and I could not have been more satisfied with the decisions taken and the results of these decisions,' he said.

It had been Charles' responsibility to convince the powers that be of the vital importance of running the race on Monday. There were quite a few amongst the police hierarchy who had doubted the wisdom of this plan and who had initially felt it most unlikely that there would be sufficient time available to guarantee the total safety of the course. 'All credit to the police as they backed us all the way when they were aware of the significance of the race being run. Frankly, what they achieved in the time they had was miraculous,' he said.

Sunday is still all a bit of a blur for Charles but he does clearly remember the morning press conference at police HQ and the subsequent press conference with the racing press at our temporary press centre in the Park Hotel. 'Arriving back at the course was a pretty unnerving experience,' recalls Charles. 'Seeing all those trainers and jockeys waiting anxiously in the Melling Road was very humbling. Later on that day, at about 6.15, I recall very clearly the critical meeting I had with Andrew, Richard and Julian when we reviewed and finalised our plans for the next 24 hours. I guess this was our key meeting of the whole weekend.

Not long after Charles had arrived back, Ian Renton and Peter Daresbury went to talk to the trainers and jockeys at the Horsebox Park entrance and after discussions with the police it was agreed that those who could be identified and who had their car keys could be admitted and allowed to drive away.

'This did not help the poor jockeys though,' explained Ian. 'Their keys, money and clothes were still in the weighing room, so once again it was back to police control to request another concession. These constant distractions must have been infuriating for the police but they were again very understanding and agreed to allow a small party to cross to the changing rooms under escort. There we gathered together all we could and returned to the car park where the jockeys, with the help of their association secretary Michael Caulfield, were able to retrieve a lot of their belongings and, in particular their car keys. We also returned the kit for Monday's meeting at Kelso, which a desperate valet continuously reminded us would be abandoned if he was not able to get the bag back.'

Richard Thomas had been busy dealing with Charles Barnett's tough request for 300-plus security guards. Anyone who knows Richard well will be aware of his great ability to make major tasks seem like small ones, something he could well have learned from John Parrett, who possessed a similar talent. As a consequence, not too long after Richard arrived on site at 8.30, close to 325 turned up, in uniform, ready for duty. 'This was a great effort by Ian Bridge and his organisation Special Projects,' said Richard. 'Quite a number who arrived had been at the racecourse on Saturday and others had been at Old Trafford. Furthermore I was delighted to see that the security force were all armed with radios and fully charged batteries.'

On Sunday morning Haydock Park was encountering some security problems of its own and naturally it was down to Richard to resolve these too. Racecourse stables are very much a restricted area, quite probably and quite properly the most restricted area on the course. However when the trainers arrived there on Sunday the stables resembled Old Trafford when United are home. TV and radio crews, press men and women, and plenty of members of the general public, all endeavouring to find out about the well-being of the contenders. Richard was able to deal with this with a few phone calls. The stables were cleared and the hostel restricted to lads only (some evacuated racegoers had camped there overnight) and the trainers were left to tend their charges and concentrate on the job in hand.

Julian Thick had to use Inspector Laidler's password to gain admission on Sunday morning. 'One of my main jobs was to organise the bagging up of all personal belongings from private boxes, hospitality areas and all the bars,' he said. 'We carefully labelled everything and made sure that we knew where all items had been found. The police insisted that we were accompanied by a Special and the task took us through the night into the early hours. It was an amazing sight, as though everyone had gone to the loo at the same time. I doubt I shall ever see anything like it again.'

Probably one of the best tales of the weekend concerns the last entry in a hospitality box visitors' book discovered by Julian late into Sunday night. The last entry read as follows: 'Name: Sergeant Somebody. Company: POLSA Squad. Comment: No Bombs Here!'

Another Sunday story and one with a happy ending, concerns Bill Wilde, whose company Special Events Parking, amongst other things, looks after admissions and cash control during the race meeting. Bill was beside himself with the loss of a box of takings containing upwards of £40,000. He was desperate, convinced that this could mean the end of his company if, as he feared, the nature of the loss would not be covered under his insurance. In fact a security guard had been sitting on the box most of the night and it had ended up in the safe keeping of Inspector Ken Laidler. Ken was as anxious to get rid of the box as poor Bill was to find it. Julian remembers the incident very well as the money had to be counted and signed for. The actual amount was, believe it or not, £44,444 exactly. Bill, as you can imagine, felt as though he had won the pools.

Apart from securing the site, Richard Thomas had another major Sunday job in hand. He was due to ride in a point-to-point at nearby Knutsford and knowing Charles was now back on site, sanity prevailed and he decided to go ahead with the commitment. In view of the shortage of time he was offered a helicopter and the police were agreeable to it taking off and landing later on at the racecourse. On arrival at Knutsford, having never seen the course before, a fence hopping tour in the chopper ensued (with the permission of the stewards). Regrettably it was to little avail as Richard finished second on the well-backed favourite Paper Field. He has assured me that the traumas of Aintree had no bearing on his performance. Both he and his mount had done their best.

When he arrived back shortly after 5 p.m., the exercise of bagging up belongings was well under way. Also racegoers were now being allowed in to collect their cars and the police had set 11 p.m. as the latest recovery time on Sunday. Thereafter all cars were to be removed and reparked in the Steeplechase Enclosure on the other side of the Melling Road. 'Julian and I watched some of this activity from the top of the Queen Mother Stand,' says Richard. 'It was an incredible sight involving over 20 towing trucks, and was really eerie seeing the lights and watching all these cars being slowly towed away. Julian and I worked through the night and although we had nothing to eat, when moving around the site there was no shortage of liquid refreshment.'

Earlier in the evening Richard had made the long hike with a police escort to the top of the County Stand to recover Peter O'Sullevan's gear. The maestro had been convinced that some of his most prized belongings would have gone missing and had arrived at the course in the early evening determined to recover all that he could. He had been able to convince the police of the importance of the matter particularly as without his gear, his 50th commentary due to take place at 5 p.m. the next day would be jeopardised. Thankfully Richard found everything intact, and returned it to a grateful and relieved Peter.

Ian Renton got to his bed at around midnight on Sunday but awoke at 2 a.m. and decided to dress and head off back to the course. 'I walked the course at 3.30 a.m.; I needed to do this before the next police search sweep which I knew to be scheduled at dusk. Having checked it out with Peter Daresbury and Dick Saunders, the chairman of the stewards' panel, I authorised watering of the course. Charlie Brooks, who was very keen for rain for soft ground specialist Suny Bay, just could not believe we had been able to organise watering. Sadly for him the ground did not soften up very much and the National was run on good to firm ground.'

For Ian, much of the remainder of Monday morning was spent in his car ringing trainers and jockeys and their agents advising them of the various arrangements in respect of off-site parking and transport. 'I was delighted with the reception I received, everyone was very supportive and determined to get the show on the road.'

On Monday morning Andrew Tulloch arrived back soon after

first light and again set about the task of working with the various contractors to prepare Aintree for racing. This must have been a monumental task as apart from keeping tabs on the various operational heads, movement was still very restricted as certain key areas had still not been given the all clear by Mark Sutcliffe and his search teams.

Briefing sessions were held with Silver Command and the contractors and arrangements were made to escort cleaners, caterers, BBC personnel, and Racetech crews to various key areas to enable them to prepare for the race to come. The cleaners, for example, had to clear all public areas and boxes, which of course, were long since empty of personal belongings, to enable the search teams to make their final thorough sweep after which that area would be sealed off and manned by a security guard. 'We finished the job just before 2 p.m.,' says Andrew. 'This was an hour later than our target deadline but it was still amazing that Mark Sutcliffe was able to hand back the course with the total confidence that it was now safe to admit members of the public.' Aintree was now ready to run the first ever Monday National.

For Richard Thomas and Julian Thick, Monday was all about keeping the site secure until the police had given the all clear. 'We managed to commandeer a BBC buggy which helped us enormously,' said Thomas. 'On one occasion we bought 120 or so burgers, stacked them on the back of the buggy, drove around the site and fed anyone who looked hungry. Some had been hard at it for 36 hours and some had had little or nothing to eat. We were not exactly offering *haute cuisine*, but it was mighty welcome, I can tell you.'

Charles Barnett describes Monday as 'an extraordinary day, and nothing like any other Martell Grand National day. Richard and Julian had set up the most thorough of security operations and I, like everyone else, was searched on entering the racecourse at the horsebox park gates on the Melling Road. There were moments on Monday when I wondered whether we would be ready but everyone was being driven by the same desire and determination. The alarm in the County Stand shortly after contractors had been admitted was a nightmare as we had to order another evacuation, but thankfully that was short-lived.'

The police had been convinced that they would receive some calls on the Monday and when they did they were almost received with a sense of relief. 'We were not aware whether they were coded although it was evident that they were being taken very seriously indeed. Several searches were carried out, including some stables and the areas around the weighing room, the parade ring, and unsaddling enclosure. As the calls had identified the exact locations, once they had been re-searched, Mark Sutcliffe and his teams were certain that the areas were sterile.'

As far as Ian Renton was concerned the last hour was just like a normal National. The atmosphere in the jockeys' changing rooms was wonderful. 'We allowed the horses into the parade ring as late as possible and then it was on to the course for the parade, preceded as always by the nerve tingling fanfare. The rest as they say, is history.'

The success of the race gave Julian Thick 'an incredibly warm feeling'. Julian has an enormous affection for Aintree. 'Unless you have been involved in the staging of the National you simply have no idea of the enormity of the task. Believe me, the Derby is kids' stuff compared with the National,' he said. In his office at Kempton Park, Julian proudly displays a beautiful print of Aintree Racecourse.

Richard Thomas just wanted to get home when it was all over. 'The drive from Aintree to my house normally takes 35 minutes but on this occasion it took me nearly three hours! I kept falling asleep, then finding myself driving down roads I'd never ever seen before. I remember saying to myself "Why has this road changed, this never used to be a dead end!"' Considering what he had been through since Sunday morning it was hardly surprising that he was out on his feet.

When Monday's race was over and a crowd of 20,000 plus, all admitted free, had witnessed another great Martell Grand National, Charles Barnett naturally felt deep satisfaction that racing had won the day. Strangely, he is amazed by the level of praise that was thrust upon Aintree. It is almost with a sense of pride that Charles recalls his belief that the 1997 Monday Martell Grand National was the first ever mainland event to go ahead on schedule following the receipt of bomb threats of this nature.

'It is rather difficult to recall the key memories that will stay with me but I can say how delighted I felt for Martell who, as in 1993, had stood by us when we most needed their support. I would be lying if I were not to admit to wondering on one or two occasions whether this would be the end of their sponsorship but, as always, they did not fail us.

'The period in my office from about 3.15 to 3.45 on Saturday afternoon was pretty tense, and the total exhaustion on Andrew Tulloch's face when he arrived at Peter Daresbury's very late that night hit me pretty hard too.

'After the meeting, the sight of the sackloads of mail which soon started arriving at the course, containing returned tickets for a 50 per cent refund was very depressing. I could not imagine how my office staff would cope. Having spent upwards of three months selling and sending out badges they now had to face a similar period sorting each and every application and returning money to all bona fide claimants.'

The task facing the Aintree office staff was mind-boggling. Sacks of mail started arriving twice daily from 9 April. Jo Pearson, who heads Aintree's badge operation, takes up the story. 'During that first week there were about ten people in the office who were not involved in the lost property operation,' she said. 'Everyone spent all day opening the mail and sorting badge refund requests into huge piles by badge type. Temporary staff who had been employed for the final build-up to the National were kept on and others brought in to help. By the second week we had two people who opened and sorted the mail and this took them all day. The checking operation then started whereby each badge was checked by serial number which enabled us to ascertain where and when each badge had been sold and whether the claimant was in fact the purchaser. The same exercise was separately completed for all our hospitality sales and together we completed the checks by the end of June. It had taken us nearly two months.

'We discovered just over 300 discrepancies and we wrote to all these to ask how the badge had been purchased. Only 50 per cent replied. We had about 250 claims against complimentary badges and we had our fair share of forgeries, all of which were forwarded to the police. The most outrageous of these was two separate sets of Tattersalls tickets with their corners cut off thus attempting to make them look like a higher value County Lawn badge. When questioned, the owners insisted that "the kids had been messing around since the event."'

It is sad that even in these stressful and unfortunate circumstances there were mindless members of the public who felt that this was an opportunity to make a dishonest financial gain. Maybe if they found themselves in similar circumstances they would be less inclined to cheat.

Aintree was refunding 50 per cent of the purchase price of each badge and in the final analysis more than £320,000 was returned to customers and this represented nearly 25,000 individual badges. You really need a dedicated team to have processed this with such care and diligence, and this is precisely what Charles Barnett has working for him.

Alongside badge refunds Aintree also had to deal with the mammoth task of returning the thousands of items of lost property. These, you will recall, had been collected by a team of Aintree staff and Specials under the direction of Julian Thick throughout Sunday night. Simone Roche was part of Julian's team and, from the Tuesday after the National, took administrative control of the return of what she had painstakingly helped tag and bag up. All the belongings had been separated into bags carefully identifying their location. They were taken away by the police on Sunday night but unfortunately when they were returned to the racecourse on Monday a lot of the bags had burst open, which resulted in another major re-sorting job.

Aintree had organised six Portakabins to be sited on the County Stand car park alongside the Ormskirk Road and with the help of Lynn Wall and the Aintree Sign Shop, large banners were hastily made identifying which Portakabin was housing what location's property. It had been announced that property collection could take place on Monday and this was administered by Gail Brown who, in her capacity as a freelance racing PR consultant, is employed by Aintree to look after owners and trainers, a job she also performs for Glorious Goodwood and several other courses.

Gail drew the short straw on Monday but believe me there would be no one better to handle this extremely tricky situation. Simone moved into the fray on Tuesday morning.

'We needed to make everything as user friendly as we could,' says Simone. 'We made a reception area and provided tea and coffee for all those who arrived in a steady stream to collect the things they had been forced to abandon what seemed an eternity ago. We tried to sort everything the best way we could and started to make a detailed inventory. We used duplicate books to record every conversation and transaction.'

Most people were apparently very understanding but Simone recalls two particular customers who she is able to laugh about now, but certainly did not do so at the time. 'One guy got really irate by the fact that we could not find his Heineken umbrella. Even though it was most probably a freebie anyway, he really created and would simply not accept that it was not there. However, even worse was the gentleman who got really aggressive because we did not have his betting slip. How on earth he expected us to either have recovered betting slips or to be able to identify their owners accurately is quite beyond me, but he got very angry and unpleasant. It was lucky for him that he was on the telephone.'

Apart from the visitors and phone calls, the Aintree staff also did their fair share of sleuthing and were able to track people down via such things as gas bills, credit cards and library tickets and by the end of the week between 85 and 90 per cent of all property had either been collected or returned by registered post or courier.

'It was interesting how we developed relationships with people over the phone,' said Simone. 'What's in your bag? What did you have in your coat pocket? How long was the strap? Some of the questions had to be quite personal but nobody seemed to mind too much. Some people were quite embarrassed, maybe they shouldn't have been there. Some even used different names, but it was not our business to pry. One particular gentleman reluctantly claimed his coat by correctly identifying a pair of tights in the left hand pocket. Naturally we didn't ask him for any further explanation.

'Sadly we also had some false claims but to the best of my knowledge we did not send or hand over someone else's property. It would have been difficult because we were very careful to ensure that everything was properly identified.'

Peter Daresbury was naturally delighted with the final outcome and with the performance of his team. 'The backing we received from the Princess Royal and the Home Office was tremendous and the efforts of the police and the emergency services were magnificent.' Peter concluded by paying tribute to his Managing Director, Charles Barnett.

Claude Duval in *The Sun* rightly billed Charles as having a 'barnstormer' and for Aintree's modest supremo, the most lasting and pleasurable memories are the magnificent support his team received. 'This came from so many quarters,' he said. 'The Princess Royal, our sponsors Martell, the trainers, the BBC, the racing industry as a whole, the police, the people of Merseyside and, most of all, our staff and those from all our contractors who came up trumps when it really mattered.'

3

The Trainers

THE relationship between racecourses and jump trainers is often a difficult one. The difficulty is more often than not caused by disagreements over reports of the going including the contentious issue of watering and what constitutes good jumping ground.

Charles Barnett and Ian Renton set out to anticipate the problems facing the trainers and were absolutely determined that they would pass going reports on at every conceivable opportunity and make themselves available whenever humanly possible to speak to the trainers. Moreover a system was set up whereby we faxed the local met office reports and forecasts direct to any trainer expressing concern over the ground. It is very important that the racecourse itself does not enter the business of weather forecasting – it's difficult enough to get an accurate picture from the experts. Amateur forecasting only leads to trouble. It would be nice to think that as a result of this strategy the trainers were able to declare their horses with the most up-to-date information available to both us and them at the appropriate time.

Despite trying, and indeed drying conditions, we were able to produce what most accepted as good jumping ground and this involved, some fairly continuous watering which, after racing on Thursday, included a Herculean all-night session by one member of our groundstaff, Tim Wain.

On Thursday, the first day of the meeting, we were able to announce good ground all round, and one highly significant factor was the decision of Lambourn trainer Kim Bailey to run Master Oats on Saturday. He declared himself satisfied with the state of the going having previously said that the 1995 Gold Cup winner would only take his chance on good ground or softer.

However, it was not the state of the ground which gave us cause for concern as we prepared for racing on Thursday. It came to our attention early in the day that horses, their connections and racegoers were experiencing severe disruption to their journeys after the closure of three motorways following a series of bomb alerts, believed to be the work of the IRA. The police had found a suspicious package on the M1 after having received an authenticated bomb threat. The M1 was closed between junctions 17 and 19, the M5 between junction 1 and the M6 link, and the M6 between junctions 7 and 10. This mindless action had inevitably resulted in chaotic scenes on roads throughout the affected areas and well beyond.

Our concern was whether horses would arrive in time for racing, particularly the first race although we took comfort from the fact that a great number of the day's runners had arrived quite early and had missed the problem. Champion trainer Martin Pipe was having serious trouble however and rang at 11.15 a.m. to say that his horse box was experiencing heavy delays and could we do anything to speed up their arrival. Martin had six scheduled runners including Nordic Prince in the first. The Merseyside police once again proved up to the task and arranged for an escort to pick up Martin's box on the M6 and this ensured the horses arrived in time to declare to run.

I can remember talking urgently to both Charles Barnett and Ian Renton at around 1.00 p.m., as I had received questions from the press room as to the possibility of a delay to the first race. After some radio calls to Derek Thompson, our stable manager, we were able to ascertain that all nine runners in the first race were safely installed in the stables so racing would go ahead on schedule. In the final analysis only two horses failed to make it through the motorway madness: Fasil, in the fifth race travelling from Wantage, and Making Time in the sixth from Brackley.

The highlight of Thursday's programme was a first Aintree treble for David Nicholson. There was no clear leader in the

London Club's top jockey table with each of the seven races being won by a different rider.

The ground remained good on Friday (thanks to Tim Wain's all night efforts) and after a tremendous day's racing David Nicholson had notched another two winners and Richard Dunwoody had stormed to a memorable treble, increasing his total to four and a virtually unbeatable lead in the top jockey's race – as indeed it proved to be.

One issue on which we have often received comment from our customers is the apparent lack of support that trainers give to breakfast at Aintree. We have long since tried to turn this into a real event and each year we encourage trainers to parade their National runners for the benefit of the general public and the hundreds of racing enthusiasts who make their way to the course at 7.30 on Grand National morning. Geoff Lester of the *Sporting Life* interviews connections and celebrities who attend but, in 1997, only 12 horses were made available and only a handful of trainers and jockeys were on hand to be interviewed. This is a real shame, because this could be a far more spectacular occasion and if we could be sure of greater support we could promote it much more extensively.

We lay on free bacon butties, tea and coffee, laced if required, with a complimentary Martell cognac. We have an enormous media presence and just about every TV and radio crew is there to grab a last minute colour piece, either to transmit live or to use later in the day. I hate to disappoint but in 1997 we certainly failed to supply enough material. I appreciate that certain horses are unable to handle this occasion, Party Politics was one such, but clearly we need to find a way to encourage more trainers to enter into the spirit of the occasion. We are after all in the entertainment business and as we are able to provide the stabling, and, now, excellent lads' accommodation, I don't really understand why so few trainers lend their support to what could be a very special event. Very often we have contenders in the stable yard but no one available to lead them out. This is very frustrating for everyone and not really fair on all those who have made the effort to come to the track so early.

In 1997 we tried something new, whereby we offered free bets on any horse that paraded and doubled the bet if a connection was interviewed. In this case there would be £300 going on to that particular horse to win the Martell Grand National. All winnings would be distributed to the stable staff. It would have been great to have lost the bet, as this would have generated considerable publicity. Sadly Lord Gyllene was not on parade on Saturday morning so there was no winning bet.

There are, of course, certain trainers who do play their part and one has to single out Jenny Pitman, who is on the early morning gallops year after year. If it were not for Jenny we would often have been in serious trouble. Her love of Aintree and the National is legendary and she has been rewarded with two memorable victories, still being the only woman to have trained a National winner. Jenny always makes herself available to the media and they love her, as her passion and emotion shines through – just as it did at Aintree on 5 April.

Jenny re-married in the summer of 1997, and with the greatest possible respect to her husband, David Stait, she has often said that she prefers horses to humans and has had more luck with her horses than her men! Whether this is true or not, what is abundantly clear is that she really does love horses. Therefore when antics of a mindless majority put the well-being and safety of horses at risk there is no containing her absolute anger. For those who saw her interview with Desmond Lynam a few seconds before the total evacuation of the racecourse it was difficult not to shed a tear with her.

* * * * * *

The highlight of Jenny Pitman's year is the ten minutes of magic that makes the Grand National. A wonderful operator with an edge that can terrify the bravest of fellow trainers, racecourse officials and stable workers, she also has a passion for the equine world which is recognised by racing fans and animal lovers alike. No-one expects, or wants, her to do anything else but put the welfare of her horses first.

On two occasions it is her brilliance with horses that has taken the Grand National to new levels. She is known as the First Lady of Aintree because she is undeniably so. Jenny's mark has been made many times over the years but she will be remembered forever for her two successes – and who would bet against more? Ben de Haan on the brilliant Corbiere in 1983 was her first Grand National winner which commanded attention around the world; Jason Titley's thrilling win on 40-1 shot Royal Athlete in 1995 merely served to underline an incomparable reputation. Cruelly denied a hat-trick of successes when Esha Ness led the diminished field home in the void race of 1993, Jenny headed north from her Lambourn stables determined to let nothing diminish her chances – and she had many with Smith's Band, ridden by the irrepressible double-winning jockey Richard Dunwoody, and Nathen Lad, paired with the already successful Titley.

There was, however, a nagging doubt at the back of Jenny's mind. The IRA was active and that very week her own Thursday journey to Aintree had been disrupted by the motorway incidents. 'My husband Dave and I had been discussing the whole situation,' said Jenny. 'But we thought it was unlikely they would do it to the people in racing because we've always had such a good relationship with the people in Ireland.' Sadly, Jenny's assessment was misjudged, but just how mistaken she was at that time became all too apparent in the following days. The public cataclysm that was to follow was only a part of it. Privately, there was also a sinister and chilling side to Jenny Pitman's Grand National she only now can bring herself to reveal.

David Nicholson, a master of the Aintree meeting yet still to win the greatest prize of all, was another who feared an outside influence might disturb the three days. 'Basically, I half had a feeling there could be trouble from Thursday,' David recalled from his magnificent yard at Temple Guiting. Those doubts did not take any obvious toll on the man known to all in racing as 'The Duke'; after Shankar's victory in the Cordon Bleu Handicap Hurdle, the first race on the Saturday, he had collected an incredible six winners from the meeting. It is a memory which lasts as long for him as the ensuing events. 'It was unbelievable,' he said.

Derek Thompson, the stable manager at Aintree, would

describe all Grand National meetings as unbelievable. He had been working there for 30 years in April, going right back to when Brian Fletcher won the race on Red Alligator in 1968. 'This was my fourth National as the actual stable manager,' recalls Derek. 'The stables are split into two so I have my son-in-law Michael Flynn in charge of the bottom yard, where I put the Irish horses along with Jenny Pitman's and a few others. In my top yard I have lots of comings and goings, anything up to 300 horses over the meeting and they start arriving from Ireland on the Monday.'

Derek lives on the Melling Road but for the National meeting, even that is too far to risk going in the evenings and overnight. 'I sleep in a room above the office,' he said. 'There are just mattresses on the floor. They bought me a bed a while ago but it wouldn't go up the stairs because of the banister. I cut the banister down and then it wouldn't go through the door! It's just a little box room, with nothing on the walls, but it's overlooking the stables. I don't sleep anyway. I'm waiting for footsteps, listening out.'

Derek never gets to see the race for real; as the 40 or so runners wind their way from his stables towards the parade ring and ultimately the stiffest challenge in National Hunt racing, he still has a yard bursting full of horses who have just competed in the Cordon Bleu Handicap Hurdle, the Martell Red Rum Steeple Chase or the Martell Aintree Hurdle. After the National there are another two races to complete the day's programme; they may not be the ultimate challenge of the day, but are still of enormous value to the owners, and a feather in the cap of the trainers and jockeys.

Everything was running smoothly for Derek and his team on 5 April; the hopefuls and the probables had left his immediate care to be greeted by an excited crowd of 60,000; he had checked the other horses, sent off the trainers with a wish for good luck. Everything seemed secure. 'I'd had the bomb squad checking over on the Friday night, which is normal procedure,' he said. 'I managed to grab a few minutes and I was watching the television.'

Outside his compound, Jenny, The Duke and their fellow

trainers were running through their own pre-race routines. David was wondering if it could possibly be a magnificent seventh success of the three days; Jenny hoping for her third National winner.

'I was talking to Desmond Lynam, being interviewed for the BBC,' said Jenny. 'Out of the corner of my eye I caught some activity and I wondered if there was a scuffle going on. Just for a second it distracted me from what Desmond was saying as I was thinking about what was going on. I finished the interview and went and got the tack to saddle up my two runners.'

David was a few boxes down from the First Lady in the saddling boxes, just next to the Parade Ring. 'I went out to saddle Turning Trix,' he said. 'I put the saddle on and was just putting the sheet on. The Princess Royal had been chatting a bit before and she was watching us saddle the horse and all of a sudden I saw three or four police converge. All I said to her was: "Trouble?"

"Yes, I'm afraid I'm off. I've been told I've got to leave."'

Jenny saw the bustle of activity surrounding the Princess. It brought back memories of the conversation she been through with her husband, but she still thought it was unlikely Aintree, with all its Irish traditions and links, would be threatened.

'I was saddling up Nathen Lad, because we had left him to last, and I could hear voices,' she said. 'Believe it or not when you are saddling up there is noise but not loud noise, it's like people talking quietly to each other as if it's muffled. Then I could hear these loud voices and I was thinking: "What's going on out there?"

'We were just about to go into the parade ring when we heard someone tell us to clear the area. One of the lads came in and said there'd been a bomb scare and I just couldn't believe it. For a minute I just shook my head in disbelief that it could happen.

'The security men came down and they were telling us to move the horses out of the saddling areas. Nobody had a clear indication as to what was going to happen at that stage. We didn't know where there was likely to be a bomb going off, if there was one. We hadn't got a clue. It could have been that area or anywhere. The horses that were already in the parade ring started filing out of one exit and our horses were filing out of the other and of course the crowds were going out of every exit.'

David was more relaxed. 'I went back to the weighing room, the horses were sent back to the stableyard, then my wife and I went in different directions. I kept thinking it wasn't really a problem, the race would still be on. Then it got more serious when they said that we were to evacuate the racecourse and the stands and everyone was to go into the middle.'

Jenny recalls: 'I was walking along keeping an eye on my two horses and we got held up because of the vast number of people going out of the exits. They were shipping everybody, including the horses, out of the same exits. We were trying to make our way back to the stables and we were held up for quite a while. They then got enough people to shift the horses out and they went back to the stableyards. Everybody was a bit bewildered; we put the horses back in the box and David, myself and the travelling head lad were talking about whether we should take the tack off. I said that if they were able to start the race there was no way they would let the horses go out of the security area without the jockeys re-weighing so we'd got to take the tack off them. We took the tack off them and put coolers on them and led them around for a while. I guess we were there for 15 or 20 minutes and the stable manager in the small yard said "Do you want a cup of tea". I said: 'What a brilliant idea.'''

The stable manager where Jenny's horses were being held had escaped the chaos relatively lightly; Derek Thompson was now the fulcrum of the other trainers' anxiety and frustration. 'After I had seen what was happening on the television I immediately looked for my emergency procedures, which had been changed from the day before. The horses came back with the trainers. I didn't really make any decisions immediately after the alarm went off.'

Jenny added: 'There were all sorts of rumours going around that the race was going to be abandoned. There was a small television in the office and you could see people jumping on the fences. We thought there was no way they were going to run the race that day.

'There wasn't chaos but there were one or two people not

behaving as they should. I guess it was nearly 4 p.m. and people had had a few drinks. We realised racing was extremely unlikely to take place so we decided to put the horses back in the boxes and give them a small drink.

'The next thing there was a very official policeman and a security man. I could tell he was official because he had a flat cap on and a cane and they walked into the yard and said: "Clear the area". We thought that there was maybe something in that area and we just looked at one another in total disbelief.

'My last memory of being in the stable yard that night was Nathen Lad who was looking over the door and he had a childlike look on his face, sort of pleading. He was worried and bewildered and he was looking at me as though he was saying please don't leave me. I was upset because of the way the horse was looking at me and I said: "I can't leave my horses."

'This bloke said: "You either leave or you'll be removed".

'So then I had visions of being on the front page of the newspapers, handcuffed to a couple of policemen. You could tell by his tone that we had to go. His tone was such that I was concerned that there might be something in that area and I was scared.

'It was obvious it would have been dangerous by the number of people around and everything else that was going on. You couldn't take those highly charged racehorses from that stable yard and walk them out into the horsebox car park. The safest place for them to be was in their stables. It would have been silly to have attempted to get those horses through all those people.

'As David, myself and our lads were leaving the stable yards I was upset and crying a bit. Sue Barker from the BBC saw me walking along and she said Desmond was doing an interview and he had got David Gandolfo and some of the jockeys talking about the fact there had been a bomb threat. At the time I still couldn't believe it could be the IRA. I thought it was the animal rights people. I was angry, thinking to myself how stupid can you be. I was thinking that they are animal lovers and here we have a situation where horses are bewildered and worried and frightened about a situation that they had never encountered before.

'I did an interview with Des Lynam and just as we were coming to the end of our chat Charles Barnett came along and moved Des and everybody else out of the horsebox park. That made me more concerned that there was a problem; that there was a threat to the horses.'

The Duke was more concerned about finding his wife. 'We'd parked the car in the horsebox park then we had lunch in the middle of the course between two of my owners and their cars. When the trouble started I presumed the Missus would go back to where we had lunch so I went back there, had a glass of red wine and eventually we heard the National was off. With that, and a full glass of wine in my hand, I quietly made my way back to the car park. When I got there I was not allowed near the car. I saw my travelling head lad and I asked him if he had seen my wife and he said she was at the top gate.'

Nigel Twiston-Davies, trainer of Grange Brake, Dakyns Boy and eventual third-placed Camelot Knight, spotted the trouble early and he left for his car immediately the announcement came. 'I decided there would be nicer places to have a drink so we got in the car and drove straight out. We went to a local hotel and as soon as we heard that the meeting was off we drove home to Cheltenham.'

Also lucky to make a quick getaway was Buckboard Bounce's handler Gordon Richards. 'I went straight to the car park as it was clear to me that there would be no more racing. I left very quickly, and was home at Greystoke by 6pm and had an early night.'

As the crowds, the jockeys and the trainers were ushered away from the course and the stands, Thompson was left with a diminishing team of helpers to look after more than 100 racehorses still in his care. 'When horses got back from the parade ring Ian Renton came up to me and said; 'Look, Derek, you'll have to get everyone out.' I got them all out on to Melling Road – my staff, kitchen staff, canteen girls, stable lads, the trainers. It left just me and Charles Dodd, who manages our stable lads' hostel.

'Some trainers had taken the tack off, some hadn't. I was waiting for instructions, everyone was milling around and I went round the yard and got everyone out. A lot of people didn't want to go, particularly the stable lads, who obviously wanted to stay with their horses.'

In the bottom yard, Phil Sharp and Simon Molloy, the lads looking after Suny Bay, indeed refused to leave. Partially hidden by their location, they insisted on walking around with the Charlie Brooks-trained favourite for the big race. 'They were based in the bottom yard with Jenny Pitman's lot and wouldn't put the horse in his stable,' said Thompson. 'They were walking the horse around the pre-parade ring. Everyone had cleared the area by then and Lord Daresbury came up to me and said: "Look Derek, you've got to get out".

'I was in the forces and I didn't want this lot kicking me out. I said the last thing they are going to hurt is the horses. Lord Daresbury told me to come to the gate, so I followed. When he left I went back and looked after the horses.'

Derek was frantically trying to look after his charges with little or no help. Many had just returned from competing in the Martell Aintree Hurdle and there had been no time to go through the post-race routine, taking the saddles and bridles off, rubbing them down and ensuring they stayed warm with a blanket. This almost had disastrous consequences, something which still infuriates Derek. 'There was a horse becoming ill with colic,' he said. 'Wee River, one of the runners in the Martell Red Rum Steeple Chase. The problem was some of the horses had not been cooled down, they had just been stuck in the boxes and then the lads had been kicked out. Consequently they had not been attended to.

'Wee River was in box number one and I was getting very concerned. The other horses were sweating up a bit. Fortunately I was in constant contact with the veterinaries over the radio and they told me to do whatever I wanted. They told me to take the gaiters off so I said to the lad of Suny Bay: "You know more about horses than I do. Get Suny Bay into a stable and come and help me with these."

'I told him I had a free stable in my yard and at first he refused. But some horses were still tethered to the wall and saddled up and Wee River was getting particularly ill. Another was trying to roll while still tethered.

'All the trainers were in their car park but behind a gate. I told Jim Needham, one of the veterinary surgeons, over the radio that I would go down and see some of the trainers and ask if it was all right that we tended to their horses. They were all pushing keys to the stables at me, saying: "Please look at my horse, give it some water, put a blanket on it. Feed the horses."

'I said I had two stable lads and they would help. I was using bolt cutters to cut locks off because people had locked horses in and I didn't have the key. We used to have a set of locks all exactly the same but they were about 80 years old and over the years locks have been lost or seized up and replaced and the key only opened so many. I wasn't going to spend my time looking for spare keys so I just got the bolt cutters.'

Derek was as relieved as anyone that as he came towards the end of the mission, the police, under increasing pressure from frantic trainers and owners, allowed some of the lads and trainers back into his compound. 'The vets came to attend to Wee River, who by then was in a really poor state. In the end he had to go to Leahurst Veterinary Field Station in Neston, where he was in intensive care for about three days. Fortunately he recovered and was racing again. But he was very, very ill. We nearly lost him all because of those phone calls.'

Jenny was experiencing conflicting emotions. After breaking down on television in tears, she too was ushered away. 'I know we had talked about it on the way to Aintree; about the motorways and that they were IRA threats and the code warning, but I never thought they would attack racing,' she said. 'We were standing in one of the gateways with a big, big crowd of people. It was terribly cold and you're colder because you're upset and you're shocked. There's a lot of thoughts going through your mind; thinking the race has got to go on for the sake of the country.

'By now we knew there'd been an IRA coded warning and we heard a couple of muffled explosions while we were stood there. That came from the racecourse proper and I was thinking: "God, I hope no one is injured, that there hasn't been a disaster and someone has been blown up." Then you start thinking about the security men and what a horrible job they had and the worry their families must have. Dave tried to put things in perspective from our point of view and said it was only a race.

'We stood there for three quarters of an hour or so and we were getting colder and colder. One of the funnier things was I was dying to spend a penny and there were no loos there. I crept back round the gatepost into the horsebox car park and I went along the back of the boxes, very quietly so the police wouldn't notice me, and I climbed up into our horsebox and used it for a loo. Then I got into the front seat and fortunately one of the travelling head lads had left his coat there so I wrapped that around me because I was freezing cold.

'We were there maybe two hours and people had started drifting away, saying racing had been abandoned. I had a phone call saying racing was off and what about running the race on Monday? I said I felt it was necessary for the country's sake. We decided we would walk into the town and there were thousands along the street. Fortunately we were going to stay there Saturday night so we hadn't checked out of our hotel and as we walked along the street, cold, tired, hungry and thirsty, this woman came running down the street saying "Are you Jenny Pitman?" I said that I was and it was music to my ears when she replied: "Do you want a cup of tea?". I said I could murder one.'

'We turned round and walked back up the street and they took us in and made us a cup of tea and got the biscuits out. Strangely enough the woman's husband worked for the bomb squad before he retired. They were wonderful. They knew a chap who was a cab driver and he said the town was unbelievable, choc-a-block. They tried to get a couple of cabs up but they weren't allowed where we were so it was arranged we would walk down the street and meet outside a pub somewhere.

'We set off and there were people looking out of their windows. They were coming out of the houses and saying: "Are you Jenny Pitman? Would you like to come in for a cup of tea?" It was just unbelievable. I stopped and spoke to them and said "Thanks, we're just getting a cab." The townspeople of Liverpool were angry, annoyed. They weren't raging but they were annoyed. They felt that something that was very dear to them was in danger of being destroyed. It was typical of the northern hospitality that they wanted to repair some of the damage and do what they could for the people who had been stranded.

'We got the cabs and went back to the hotel. By that time there was a string of messages from newspaper reporters, from TV, from radio, from people who wanted to chat. I really felt very down at that time and I felt it was important that we were strong for one another. Although I was tired and depressed I felt that it wasn't a situation that could just be left to others. Because we had won the Grand National twice I think people wanted to know what we felt about it. David said just leave it and look after yourself for a bit because otherwise you're going to be ill. But I felt it was important. You can't say to people on the one hand stand up and be counted and on the other hand turn round and say you can count everybody else but don't count me.'

The Duke, by this time, was feeling very pleased with himself, and not just because of his incredible success that weekend. After the evacuation a few of us went into one of the houses just off the Melling Road, making phone calls. I rang the hotel where we were staying. I told them we were coming back there. They told me: "We've got no beds". I said: "I don't give a bugger what you've got, but we're coming."

'By then we were thinking we had to do something regarding the horses. I spoke to a high-ranking police officer and said: "Look, I can entertain all these people here if you'll let me. There's a bootful of booze in that car, which we've won, magnums of this that and the other, the lot."

'He said: "You can't go near it."

'"Fine, I am only trying to help". Mind you, I could have done with a bloody jar myself!

'My assistant trainer was fortunate because he had gone straight back to his car and got out. The travelling head lad, the Missus and I were pressing the police a bit, saying: "You've got to get these horses out."

'Not long after we saw the horses start to load up so we went to our car. The police were more interested in overseeing the horses so we managed to drive out between two horseboxes. The police tried to stop me but I told them I was going. We did well to get out. I still had the same glass that I had from the middle of the racecourse; empty though by this stage.'

Simon Earle was the trainer of leading contender Dextra Dove who in quite a few people's eyes stood a very good chance of grabbing some National glory. After the evacuation Simon was given permission to keep his horses – he also had an intended runner in the bumper – at Aintree.

He explained: 'Dextra Dove had a terrible journey up from Dorset on Thursday as we were affected by the M6 bombs. On arrival it became apparent that he hated the change of water and I was reluctant to move him again with the strong possibility of the race taking place in the very near future. Eventually we were given permission to take the horses away but as mine were staying I filled the box with people instead and set off for the hotel in Runcorn. We had a really good meal and plenty to wash it down with although I was concerned to see Chris Maude gorging himself, particularly as he weighed out 3lb overweight on Saturday. To be fair to him, he starved himself for the rest of the weekend and when the time came on Monday he hit the scales spot on 10 stone.'

For Jenny Pitman, the nightmare was only just beginning. She was trying to relax in her hotel when some devastating news arrived: a death threat. 'I got a call from home,' she recounts. 'There had been an unpleasant phone call there from somebody allegedly associated with the people responsible for the bomb. My dad was there on his own with the housekeeper and I was concerned for them. They had said: "Tell her to watch what she says because we are watching her."

'That frightened Dave to death. My sister Mandy rang up and spoke to Dave; she was crying her eyes out. I realised that whatever I felt about it, I was becoming very angry. Now I am even more angry because people had threatened me. Dave said then that it was not just myself I had to think about and that put things in the right perspective.'

Jenny was already aware that being so high-profile in the racing world, there was always a chance she could be targeted. 'I had numbers to ring,' she said. 'The threat was dealt with in a very, very professional manner.'

In the hotel, her husband and colleagues did their best to make her feel at ease. 'My assistant Paul Price, who's 22 carat gold, stayed with Dad at the house and the security people were just brilliant,' she recalled.

It was not, however, enough to subdue the spirit and defiance of Jenny Pitman. She continued her ambassadorial role for the sport. Her horses had been taken to Haydock for the night and, without a hint of the trauma she was going through, Jenny did an interview for television. No one could have guessed what was going on in her mind.

It was the same on Sunday morning. 'We were inundated with people wanting to do interviews,' she said. 'I had made up my mind there was no way I was going to be bullied or blackmailed into not saying what I felt despite the fact that I'd had this threat and despite the fact I realised I had a responsibility to my family. So I did the TV interviews. What was lovely was our farrier, Gary Pickford, and one of his apprentices, a big lad called Micky Towell, had gone up to Aintree to watch the National. On the Sunday morning they said they would come up with me to the course and try and get their car.

'My first interview was at 7.30. I told Gary they had already announced that no-one would get their cars out of the course until after lunch. They said they would try and blag it out. Then it occurred to me that wasn't why they were going up there at 7.30 in the morning. They hadn't got a hope of getting their car out.

'I had seen them and Dave in a little huddle. We all went in the same taxi and when we got out there was one of them walking on one side, one walking the other side and the third was walking in front of me. I am not joking, I was walking up the street and kept falling over with them all around me.

'I said: "What is going on here? Will you get out from under my feet!" And I started laughing because Micky Towell had got a blue coat on. I said to him: "If you keep walking around like that you'll look like a proper security man." I just wanted him to know I wasn't a fool and I knew what was going on. It made me feel very warm that they were obviously concerned for me and they were prepared to stand shoulder to shoulder with me.

'We moved the horses back to Aintree on Sunday night. On

Monday I got up and did some more TV interviews. On the racetrack itself you could still see an awful lot of litter. I thought they still had a lot of ground to make up and it was amazing. By the time we got there for the race it was like someone had waved a magic wand and it had all disappeared.' Aintree had approached First Leisure who readily agreed that the Paradox club land on the Ormskirk Road could be used as a car park for owners and trainers on the Monday. Said Jenny 'We knew we couldn't take the cars right up to the entrance and they organised it very well with the buses and so on. We met in the Manhattan Square pub and they looked after us well but I felt a bit fidgety because I wondered what was going to happen that day. I was worried about the horses because I felt they were still well but had lost a bit of their sparkle.

'I had been well chuffed with them on the Saturday, they were on the button. I felt it was like cooking a soufflé. You've cooked it and it's peaked and you're ready to eat it and then you've had to take a phone call and it's just gone a little bit. I felt we had just lost the edge.

'We walked about a mile up the course and by the time we got there there was a queue of people waiting to be searched and to go in. Somebody spotted us and we got in quite quickly.

'There was only one other thing that made me think there were still problems on the Monday. Again I was doing an interview. Des Lynam and I saw these people walking about on stilts. I thought they were not there for entertainment. In my mind I felt there must have been a problem, we'd have to keep our heads down and keep going. I looked at this bloke and I thought "You're not an entertainer." I thought what better place to be to see what's going on than on stilts.

'Although I didn't feel very chirpy I tried to be as normal as possible for everybody's sake. At the end of the day I'm just the captain of the ship and if you have a few problems it's my responsibility to keep the ship afloat. The horses were getting quite wound up because they had been through a situation on the Saturday they couldn't equate to. There was a bit of unease but you felt you had to bite the bullet and get on with it. We had to keep out heads down and just get on with the job.'

There was another shock in store for Pitman when the race was eventually run. Smith's Band was amongst the leaders and jumping superbly under the guidance of Richard Dunwoody when tragedy struck at the 20th fence.

'We lost Smith's Band there,' she said. 'On reflection, in my opinion the horse died as he picked up. I think he had picked up and had a heart attack. That's happened to us on the gallops before, to young horses. There's no doubt he had a heart attack. It could have happened in any race but it was unfortunate it happened at Aintree.

'It made the situation from our point of view even sadder but the racecourse people and the vet dealt with it in such a professional way. I knew the horse was dead, there was nothing I could do. We'd gone up to the stable yard and I said to the vet: "Whatever you do I want the horse back". They made arrangements to have him cremated and he came home. That makes me feel better about it.'

David Nicholson still looks back with satisfaction at his Six of the Best. And he smiles when he recounts the good-natured banter that started after the weekend. 'A story started that I had planted a bomb on the Thursday morning to stop Martin Pipe getting there,' he said. 'And he planted a bomb on the Saturday to stop us having any more bloody winners!

'I had no problems with how the police handled the situation. They had a job to do and a code of conduct and rules to follow. I don't think they over reacted at all. There were bombs on the M1 and the M6 so they couldn't take any risks. Not at that sort of occasion.

'I actually wanted them to run the race on the Sunday but of course they couldn't. When it did take place, the atmosphere was superb. I thought it was two fingers to them from the racing people, the general public, you name it. Everyone turned up on the Monday, including Flat trainers – a whole load of them from Newmarket. Everybody came to support the sport of racing.'

The weekend was a blur for Derek Thompson. On Saturday evening the last of those horses which were to be moved left at 7.30 p.m. 'We were still arguing with the police until about 11 p.m. because they were still trying to get rid of the lads. All the horses went in the end except Simon Earle's and the Irish,' he said. 'I was watching the television at about one in the morning and Julian Wilson was on television saying all the horses had left Aintree and gone to Haydock, local stables or gone home. But nine were still there.

'I wanted to get a policeman to stick on the gate so I could get a couple of hours sleep but they had other priorities. So about 1.30 in the morning I thought I would go and try and find one. I left the stable yard and walked all the way round to the weighing room and the offices and there wasn't a single person. I didn't bump into one person. All the champagne was on the tables, the coats and everything.

'In the end I walked down to the police control room and said I had been all around and there wasn't a soul in sight. They said I wasn't supposed to go round there. It hadn't been cleared yet.

'Sunday was my biggest problem because all the horses had been evacuated apart from the Irish and I had no clean boxes left and I had to get my staff in to clean them up for when they arrived back on the Monday. But the police wouldn't let anyone in so I had to go to the gate myself. Everyone was screaming at me at the gates to get them let in so they could get their cars. There was nothing I could do.

'On the Sunday the Merseyside mounted police brought me a load of feed for the horses but Arthur Moore has special food and he was flying it in from Ireland. I had to arrange to get it from Liverpool airport. The helicopter division of the police said they couldn't get it because they weren't landing on the course. It came in with Ryan Air. I worked with Royal Mail for 25 years and they have a depot at the airport and they agreed to pick it up and send it along here.'

Thompson also ensured he gained his own little piece of revenge for the chaos caused. 'I made sure the Press got the story about Wee River,' he said. 'One of the horses nearly died because of what they did. I told them to make sure they printed it so they didn't get away with it. I didn't want them damaging my horses. Stupid people like that causing horses to suffer.'

4

The Jockeys

A JUMP jockey's life is a hard one and I am sure the good days are well outweighed by the bad. Pushing a tired body through a three-mile chase with an unwilling partner, quite possibly in driving sleet or icy rain, has got to be worth a lot more than the riding fee of under £90. It is also quite possible the jockey will have driven many miles to take that ride, in which case anything less than a win will, in all probability, mean a considerable loss on the day.

Heavy falls are an accepted part of the job and a jump jockey knows that every time the tapes go up the risk is there and there is a chance the day could end in pain, either in the racecourse hospital or in a local infirmary. Despite all this, jump jockeys turn out day after day in search of rides and hopefully winners, to provide entertainment to the racegoers and betting opportunities to all those at the course and in the thousands of betting offices throughout the United Kingdom.

The Grand National has often been described as the greatest test of horse and rider. Run over four-and-a-half miles with 30 of the most testing fences anywhere in the world, it requires extreme resilience and courage but perhaps strangely is not a race with a history of serious injury to the jockey. Neither, of course, is the Grand National the dangerous race for the horse that many would have you believe. Naturally there are fatalities and everyone deeply regrets them when they occur, but at Aintree we are extremely upset when any incident in any of the 19 other races at the meeting is immediately attributed to the National and is used against us by those who wish to do the race harm. Merely riding in the National is an aspiration of every jump jockey and there can be no doubt where they would most like to be at around three o'clock on Grand National day.

The final build-up to the big race is a wonderfully exciting moment. Butterflies flutter deep down in the stomach, banter is exchanged, last gasp drinks are hurried down and final adjustments are made to colour and clothing. Anxious valets check that everything is in place. Assistant Clerk of the Course Ian Renton will be about to visit the hallowed changing rooms to brief the jockeys telling them how to prepare for the parade, not to rush down to the first, not to bunch up – together with a host of 'what happens if' situations. All the jockeys will listen attentively, they will know this is for real, they know the challenge that lies ahead, they'll need all the help they can get.

The jockeys' changing rooms at Aintree are something to behold, a relic from the Victorian age, steeped in stories and the greatest traditions of the sport. The senior jockeys occupy the prime berths and as a result tend to be chatting together. Once the call comes for the long walk to the parade ring under the eyes of the unobtrusive BBC cameras, there's no turning back; it is time to meet the owner and receive last-minute instructions from an apprehensive and often nervous trainer. Then it's: 'Will jockeys please mount' and the long walk to the Grand National start begins.

This time the visit they are all expecting never comes and, when Ian Renton does arrive, it's to tell them to evacuate the area. There has been a bomb threat and within minutes the changing rooms are deserted – as the BBC cameras so stunningly revealed.

The jockeys, along with trainers, owners and other officials made their way to their car park, most of them dressed just in their racing silks and breeches. The lucky ones amongst them had time to grab a jacket or light coat but very few left with car keys, credit cards or cash or the most crucial piece of a jockey's equipment, the mobile phone. In some ways, the absence of the mobile proved a real bonus as it enabled them to have a relatively relaxed time away from the constant interruptions and questions that usually dog their weekends.

Charles Barnett and I had once again been down at police HQ

attending a mid-morning press conference. Everyone seemed to be there: BBC, Sky, ITN, plus many familiar faces and lots of our friends from the racing press corps. It was here that Charles was able to confirm that the Martell Grand National would be run at 5 p.m. on Monday, subject only to final police clearance. The whole occasion seemed so unreal, yet everyone was of one mind – the show must go on.

After the press conference it was back to the course. This time the journey took a more realistic 15 minutes or so. As we arrived on the outskirts of the course my heart sank. People were everywhere, all looking lost and anxious, litter was strewn across the Ormskirk Road and there were police cordons whichever way you looked. Our meeting point was at the rear of the horsebox park, adjacent to the BBC outside broadcast vehicles. To reach there we took the short drive down the Melling Road. We were cleared through the police roadblock and as we passed the entrance to the car park I could not believe my eyes. There, like lost souls, were such famous names as Josh Gifford, Nicky Henderson, Toby Balding, Richard Dunwoody, Carl Llewellyn and Jamie Osborne along with many other colleagues.

Charles and I agreed that helping these guys had to be a major priority – and one that should be tackled immediately. Ian Renton was on-course and he and Lord Daresbury went to talk to the trainers and jockeys to assure them that we would be doing all we could to get them away as soon as possible. Soon afterwards it was agreed with the police that as the car park was now a sterile area, having been fully checked over by the search teams, we could admit individuals to collect their cars, provided they could produce their keys and we could identify them personally.

Nicky Henderson was first in and after being body searched was into his car and off – I well remember a few celebratory toots as he left. So followed the slow process of freeing up more and more cars to enable the racing professionals to go about their business and, more particularly, get back to their horses. It was strange, but seeing the faces of such famous racing names straining against the gates reminded me of Pathé News footage of PoW camps. Why it did I don't know, but that's what came to mind.

Our problem was doubly difficult with the jockeys as they had left the changing rooms in their silks, mostly with no coats, no money, no credit cards, and most vitally in the present circumstances, no car keys. All their belongings were left behind in the changing rooms and they were in an area of the racecourse which, as well as the press room, had not been thoroughly searched. Michael Caulfield, the ever diligent and professional secretary of the Jockeys Association was soon on the case and with Ian Renton, arrangements were made with the police to permit a small group to be escorted across the deserted concourse to the changing rooms to gather up all jockeys' belongings, and valets' holdalls (one containing most of the kit for Kelso's race meeting on Monday) and bring them all to the car park. All the jockeys were permitted to enter, and identify their gear and possessions, to collect their cars and leave. They returned on Monday for the real battle.

*   *   *   *   *

For Richard Dunwoody, winner of the Grand National on West Tip in 1986 and Miinnehoma in 1994, it was a relaxed start to such an ill-fated day – and eventually to an ill-fated Grand National itself. A veteran of many such occasions, he was not unduly worried about another weekend under the spotlight; another Saturday when millions of pounds of betting money would be staked on his name and his reputation. As it was for many years, he would be the housewives' choice to multiply their pin money, and he would be the gamblers' choice to multiply their stakes and win or lose fortunes. He had grown accustomed to such weights of expectation, and he would bear those hopes in his own relaxed style with a shy smile, a shrug of the shoulders and fierce professionalism.

Richard was due to ride Smith's Band in the big race, trained by Jenny Pitman. After a typically early alarm call at his hotel in Haydock, he left his girlfriend Emma Heanley and was cantering on his mount by 6.30 a.m.

'I just wanted to loosen up his legs a bit before the race,' said Richard. 'There was quite a crowd there already. I was looking forward to the race and Jenny Pitman was pleased with his form even though he'd had only one run and been pulled up. In every other respect things were looking pretty good.'

Richard, three times champion jockey now enjoying the early twilight of his career in the saddle, picking and choosing when and where to ride, was in more demand than most for his views on the National. There were interviews for him and Jenny with Sky and with various radio stations before he could start focusing on the real business ahead.

'Before I could think about riding I had about three pounds in weight to lose because I wanted to get down to 9st 10lb or 9st 13lb,' he said. 'I actually once lost about six or seven pounds before a Whitbread so it was nothing out of the ordinary but I still needed to get back to the hotel and sit in a hot bath.

I was in there for about 45 minutes and I like to get to the course early to avoid the traffic and so on. I arrived at about 10.30 and immediately walked the course to get out of the weighing room and out of the way of all that is happening on such a big occasion.'

While Richard went through his much-rehearsed routine, Michael Caulfield was spending time by the grave of his father. Judge Caulfield, a keen horseman who used to ride out at local stables, died a couple of years before, and Michael would take the chance to remember; to spend some time tidying in the St Helens' cemetery. It was a rare chance to be alone with his thoughts before one of the highlights of his year. 'My father's family are from St Helens, from Haydock,' he recalls. 'I have a great feel for the race as I grew up with stories of the Grand National. I arrive on the Friday afternoon of the meeting, and on Saturday morning the first thing I do is go to visit my father's grave, take some flowers and tidy up. It is a very poignant weekend for me and I drive around where I spent a lot of my youth before heading for the track.

'I arrived at Aintree at around 11.30 a.m. and walked the course with many of the jockeys. Even that early I thought the atmosphere this time was absolutely unbelievable. We had 38 confirmed runners, the place was alive, it was an open race and perfect ground. It was set up for a thrilling National.

'It had come on the back of a great Cheltenham, no-one had been badly injured in the build-up, no dramas, the crowds on the Thursday and Friday were up. A lot of the jockeys were doing ten stone because they had been wasting all week to get somewhere on or near that mark. They had also enjoyed a cracking night in Liverpool on the Thursday; they had met Robbie Fowler for a few beers and some of them had called him Robbie *Flower*; the whole atmosphere was flying.

'After walking the course I came back to the jockeys' room and the atmosphere in there was pretty serious because they were still trying to hit the weights. Nonetheless it was Grand National day and all the racecards were being signed for the valets and everyone; it's pretty unique. The jockeys were having half a cup of tea and watching Grandstand as they broadcast the build-up; then going into the sauna, coming out for a bit of ice and then back in the sauna again.'

Dunwoody was one of the many in and out of the sauna; a place hated and dreaded by the jockeys, but one which is so necessary as they deprive and punish their bodies in the quest for the extra ounce which they hope will make the difference between victory and the heart-wrenching agony of second place. He also had the extra distraction of more interviews, this time with Desmond Lynam for *Grandstand*. A couple of visits to hospitality boxes followed before Dunwoody was allowed to prepare himself for another day's work in the saddle. 'I had two quite important rides – Celibate in The Chase and Pridwell in the big hurdle – so I was concentrating more on them at the time than the National itself,' he said. 'It helps to have a couple of rides beforehand to loosen up. It's a very different day but there are lots of routine things going on as well.'

The jockeys' room in the last minutes before the Grand National is a hive of excitement. In one room the senior riders prepare; there is a scale for final checks on their weight, antiquated benches surround a bricked-up fireplace and there is a sauna at one end. The younger jockeys are in a second room; no sauna, no showers, no toilets, just scales, a table and a few pegs to hang their clothes. In both rooms, they sit alongside each other comparing notes on their mounts, trying to pass the time and wishing each other well. Those who had ridden in the 2.55 arrive, little time to change into new colours, no chance to gather their thoughts before tackling the most daunting event on the calendar.

There was no warning of what was to follow. There were 38 of the most gifted jump jockeys gathered in two changing rooms, some standing, some sitting, some talking to themselves or to the claustrophobic atmosphere around them, some trying to relax with a last cigarette. All imagining themselves punching the air in delight after winning the greatest race of all. Outside the trainers and owners were discussing tactics for the last time; exchanging views and arguing on how to ensure their horses were to be given the best possible chance to claim the prize of a lifetime.

Michael Caulfield decided to watch the National in the changing room with the few jockeys sitting out the race. For them it is a strange mixture of emotions; regret that they are not taking part, but genuine hope for their friends tackling the frightening and dangerous fences. They will yell as loudly as the most excitable punter, they will be part of every stride on the course, feeling the thud as a colleague is unseated, the joy of a narrow escape, and the thrill of another obstacle negotiated successfully.

Michael says: 'I did not want to get in the way before they filed out to the paddock, so I was waiting outside before joining the others in the changing room. Then it happened. "Bing, bong, Operation Aintree".

'The jockeys were still waiting for their talk from Ian Renton and the stewards; a lot of them are shaking hands and wishing each other good luck. They generally just can't wait to get started, especially those on their first rides or on one of the fancied runners.'

Richard Dunwoody had little time to worry about what was ahead. 'There's more of an air of excitement than other days and some of the younger jockeys might ask for a bit of advice,' he said. 'I was one of the last to weigh out because I had ridden in the race before and I then had to change into all my light gear. I was right near the back of the queue, had literally just been on the scales and gone back into the changing room. There is a television in there and that's how we first heard that people had been told to leave the stand. We thought there might be a bit of a delay, nothing more.

'We were then told to get out of the weighing room. I had been at a course in Ireland when there was a bomb scare and we were told to leave; 20 or 25 minutes later we were back in. We thought it would be just the same, expecting to return in 15 minutes, at most an hour, but it certainly didn't turn out like that. We filed out and stood outside; Carl Llewellyn was being interviewed by Desmond Lynam and I was watching. Suddenly we were all ushered away from around the weighing room area.'

Only now did it cross the minds of those involved that this might be more than a minor irritation in their National agenda. In the confusion many scattered in different directions, bundled along by the crowds, trying to find friends, family, information; not believing what was happening.

Michael says: 'At first I thought Operation Aintree was the sign for the security and stewards at the fences to be really on their marks to make sure no one stormed the track with banners saying "Stop Jump Racing" or "Ban Hunting" or whatever it might be. Then all of a sudden police came up and told us to clear the area and I said "Certainly, officer, but you can't mean the jockeys as well?" At that point Dick Saunders, the chairman of the Stewards, came over and said; "Michael, this is serious, you have to take the jockeys out of the changing room."

'"What? In their silks?"

'"Yes. I don't know what is going on but this is really serious and you have to leave."'

Michael saw Nigel Payne running past and doing an interview with the BBC before he returned to the changing room. 'Chaps, I'm not taking the mickey,' said the jockeys' representative. 'Get out of here quickly and let's go and meet at the jockeys' car park. If I were you, I'd grab some clothes because we might be a few minutes'.

'There was still a reaction of disbelief, as if it was all unnecessary. One or two grabbed coats but some others, particularly the Irish guys, went out with their sticks and their helmets thinking they would be chucked out for five minutes and they could go straight to the paddock.'

Michael realised it was a security alert to be taken seriously especially following the M6 bomb scare. 'I was asked what I thought would happen and told them the clocks had been put forward a few days before and, knowing the resolve of the racecourse and these race people, they would want to run the

National that night if possible, even if it was at 7 p.m.,' added Michael.

Richard, amongst all the confusion, decided to walk towards the Owners and Trainers' bar and then round the back by the hospitality units and eventually towards the stables. For the most fleeting of moments, it occurred to him that perhaps, just perhaps, there was real danger to all their lives and an atrocity was about to take place. 'I suppose it was when I was walking by the hospitality area that I thought maybe a bomb was about to go off. But if it did, then so be it. There was nothing anyone could do about it.'

He gathered with many of his colleagues; Charlie Mann, Jamie Osborne and Norman Williamson were among those who had headed in the same direction. There was concern with no one able to say with any authority what was happening. 'We did another interview with Desmond Lynam and then we were told to vacate the car park by the officials and security,' said Richard. 'Charlie was about to hop in his car and leave but he left it too late and wasn't allowed to go. We went in an alleyway by the car park, then again we were told to get out and at that stage we knew the race was not going to be run that day.'

An air of resignation was setting in, but with no indication of how the next few hours would unfold. The atmosphere changed as the people surrounding Aintree opened their doors to many of the thousands milling around, offering their hospitality in a spirit defying the chaos surrounding them. Ironically, it was around 4.15, the very moment when the winner should have been triumphantly accepting his applause, when the greatest steeplechase in the world was officially abandoned.

'I had thought I might try and get away,' said Michael. 'But then, no, I would have been deserting the ship. I might be of some use, so I stood around and tried to gather some more information. I saw Dick Saunders again and said, "Sir, whenever you want to run this race, and I don't care where, whichever day, we will all be here. All these 38 jockeys will come back. End of story. It's not a question of inconvenience. Please get the race run – we can't do anything else".

'We knew by then it would not happen on the Saturday and a fair quantity of the sponsors' product – Martell – had found its way into our possession and a few glasses were being passed around, if nothing else but to keep people warm. The jockeys were wondering what on earth they could do. They were standing in their silks, had no money, no cars, no telephones.'

Richard was among the crowd and his years of experience told him to make the best of the situation. 'We ended up sitting on a wall outside the car park,' he said. 'A kind man on the Melling Road brought us out a few Budweisers. He wouldn't even give me his name when I offered to post him something but he just said don't bother. So there we were, just after the National was supposed to be run, sitting there with a can of Budweiser chatting away. It was bloody cold let me tell you!'

Despite the air of calm, the jockeys were still nervous. 'There was a bit of confusion at this stage because no one knew when we would be able to get our cars, our belongings from the course or anything,' said Richard. 'We just didn't know what to expect and we were all dressed in our silks, although I was lucky because I managed to grab my overcoat. Most of the other jockeys had absolutely nothing.

'We were making the most of our man's hospitality and then we heard that John Buckingham, the head valet, who stays at the end of the Melling Road, had a few jockeys and other people in his place so we went along and there was already a big crowd. The landlady opened her doors and we had a cup of tea and watched the news.'

Richard Dunwoody, Chris Maude, Andrew Thornton, Carl Llewellyn, Simon McNeill, Charlie Swan and Mark Richards, who had been awarded the ride on Bishops Hall in place of the injured David Bridgwater, all filed in with an assortment of wives, girlfriends, trainers and owners. J.P. McManus, the legendary gambler and owner, was another able to find refuge.

Richard was fortunate because he had already bumped into his girlfriend in the car park. For Emma, however, the journey to the Melling Road was more fraught because she was with Chris Maude's wife, Dolly, who was pregnant. 'Dolly was nervous because of her condition,' explained Emma. 'The most frightening part was when, along with thousands of others, we were trying to get through a gate past Melling Road. I wanted to get as far away from the stands as possible because if they did blow up, I was frightened that the debris could fly for miles.

'There was a helicopter overhead instructing us where to go, but at first people were still carrying on with their picnics. I recognised that the threat was real, that you couldn't take risks. Luckily we got through the gap quickly by calling out "pregnant lady, coming through".'

Many were not so lucky in tracking each other down. Richard says: 'Everyone else was looking for friends and family and some jockeys ended up in the middle of the course. Tony Dobbin rang up a friend and then walked down to the M57 motorway. On the way some little scouser on a bike rode past and said: "Hey you, only little girls wear boots like those". Tony said he nearly grabbed him off his bike and hit him!'

Fortunately for the jockeys, Michael Caulfield (known to many as 'Corky') had also found his way to John Buckingham's digs. He decided it was time to take charge and attempt to bring some order to the good-natured chaos around him. He begged hotel rooms for the jockeys in Runcorn. 'I phoned the Forte Posthouse in Runcorn and pleaded "I'm Michael Caulfield, I'm a decent bloke, and I need rooms. I will guarantee payment, although I have no way of doing so". I said we were stuck at Aintree and had no idea how we would get there, but please hold ten double rooms for us. Fortunately, she was an absolute diamond and she agreed.

'One or two of the younger jockeys then decided to drop out. They did not fancy a night out with Corky, thinking it might be a bit dull. They had been given one or two admiring glances anyway, and so they decided to head into town. I said "fair enough lads but you might regret it a bit later when you want to get some sleep", but they headed off anyway.'

The only problem left was how to get the remaining jockeys to the hotel.

'There were loads of us in there, all trying to use the phones and order taxis,' said Richard. 'The taxis looked very difficult to get hold of so we went back to the racecourse to see if anyone was leaving from there. There were a few trainers who managed to get their cars and the horseboxes were allowed to leave.'

Their timing, for once on such a day of bewilderment, could not have been better. 'Trainer Robert Alner and his wife Sally very kindly took several of us including Chris Maude, Paul Holly, Michael Caulfield, myself and others to Runcorn in the back of their horsebox, up alongside Bishops Hall! Fortunately there was plenty of standing room and again we were treated very well, diving in to their picnic basket and putting on all the weight we had taken off during the day!'

It seemed, finally, a chance to relax after the madness of the last few hours provoked by two coded telephone calls. A time to reflect on what had happened, what barbarity could have materialised, and when the National would be staged. The jockeys decided to make the most of a few hours of freedom, unpestered by mobile phones, by trainers, agents or owners. A few drinks, a dinner, and plenty of talk about the events, and how the show must go on.

'We all went off for a wash after checking in and at that point my phone rang,' said Michael. 'It was Charlie Swan and he asked me what the chances were of getting into the racecourse that night. I said: "The invisible man would have no hope. It's completely cordoned off."

'"Corky, you don't understand" said Swan. "I have to get in. J.P. McManus has left his betting cash in a private box."

'"No chance, Charlie. Forget about it and have a good night."

'Incredibly, Charlie actually managed to get in that night. He talked a CID officer into taking him to the box and recovering JP's gambling cash. No-one else but a jockey could have done that. It is the gift of the gab, the smile, the humour. It is quite extraordinary what they can get away with.'

Richard was relieved to get the chance to wind down. 'It was a good crack after what had happened,' he said. 'Although it was not quite as wild as what occurred in the overcrowded Adelphi hotel. There were plenty of stories coming out of there, including about 15 jockeys and friends in one room at the same time. Unfortunately I missed it! It sounded like a memorable evening.'

Carl Llewellyn was, indeed, part of that crowd and would not disagree with that sentiment. Many of the jockeys had spent the evening in various bars after meeting up with a hugely popular Liverpool character known as 'The Count'. He ensured his crowd were looked after for the evening as they took the rare chance to have a night on the town. The fun did not stop when they returned to the Adelphi with the night club open until gone three.

'We certainly relaxed and socialised on our diet cokes,' said Carl, with a smile. 'There were 14 people in the room I stayed in. I got there with a couple of others at 6.45 in the morning and there were ten or 11 there by then. We tried to find a pillow and as we lay down, at five to seven the door burst open and a certain Irish jockey came in with a pint of vodka in his hands and woke us all up again. We never got any sleep at all then.'

The Adelphi was the subject of a BBC documentary series, *Hotel*, and from the evidence of the programme could do with a course in customer relations. The attitude of some staff towards stunned and stranded racegoers was exploitative and unfriendly, to put it mildly. Reception staff charged for cancelled rooms – despite the fact they were filled within seconds by people from the queue begging for a place to stay. When one bedroom became vacant late on, it was auctioned, with the suggestion of £1,000 for a £95 room only said with half a smile. The Adelphi that night did open its doors to the stranded, filling many of their function rooms with grateful customers. Charging £45 for a mattress on the floor, however, hardly tallied with the spirit of the occasion.

The jockeys continued to make the most of it, many of them cramming into the hotel's tiny sauna in the middle of the night, again portraying their dedication when at that stage they were still not aware of when the National would be run. A day of disorder was followed by a morning of indecision as the jockeys gathered for breakfast. The early chatter was one of defiance, hoping the terrorists' threat would not be the winner and deprive the nation's race lovers of their favourite event.

'We read the papers and watched the news trying to keep up with what was going on,' said Richard. 'A friend of Chris Maude drove him, me and Michael Caulfield back to the course and a lot of the jockeys were trying to get their gear and their clothes, get changed and retrieve their cars. Michael was doing a lot of liaising with the police and Ian Renton, the Assistant Clerk of the Course, to get back into the weighing room and, about three hours later in mid-afternoon a group did finally manage to get back in, escorted by one of the Mersey police.'

The decision was greeted with enthusiasm by all concerned. But it did present some new concern. 'One or two jockeys jumped on to the scales when they collected their gear,' said Michael. 'The reaction was "oh, shit!" It had been that kind of night with some putting on nearly a stone. Many of them collected their cars and headed straight back to their hotels for a hot bath and sauna!'

Richard and some friends decided to first visit a point-to-point at Cheshire Forest, finding some unexpected light relief. 'There was a funny story from that day,' he recounts. 'Apparently one of the jockeys stepped off the scales, handed the saddle to someone and fell over in a heap! The police came in and breathalysed him – he was supposed to be riding in the maiden point-to-point – and he was four or five times over the limit! That was the story doing the rounds that afternoon.'

Sunday night was back to the nerves; another eve of Grand National spent thinking the race over, imagining the perfect ride and trying to dispel the thoughts of the inevitable that would befall so many jockeys and their mounts on the treacherous four-and-a-half mile course.

Richard said: 'Sunday night I went back and had a run and sauna and tried to lose a bit of weight. We had all got on the scales when we went to get our clothes in the afternoon and there were some quite heavy jockeys! Considering we had no money, no bankers' cards, absolutely nothing, we were very dependent on everyone else and had been very well looked after.

'On the Monday I got up and had some physio and went to the course. Luckily we had a car park arranged for us within ten minutes' walk. We were searched on the way in and I went into the sauna and it became clear what had been happening since Saturday. It is not the biggest of saunas at Aintree – you can fit on average seven or eight in there reasonably comfortably on two benches. At one stage on that Monday there were at least 16 jockeys in there! It was a great crack and a few stories were being relayed about the goings on over the weekend.

'It was a different atmosphere on the Monday because there were no rides beforehand, but I've always said that when you get on your horse and show him the first fence you soon know you are riding in the National. It doesn't matter what day it is, what time it is! The adrenaline soon starts going again and the preparation is much the same.

'The race itself went great – but very disappointing as far as I was concerned, of course, because we fell at the 20th. I had a very good ride until the fall. Afterwards we just gently drifted off and back to work on the Tuesday and Wednesday. I think in the same way we remember the National that never started this will stay with us for ever. It's another rich chapter in its history.'

Tony Dobbin eventually won the race on Lord Gyllene, the 14-1 shot trained by Steve Brookshaw. After such a harrowing weekend, it was one of the greatest performances by horse and rider since the inception of the great race as Lord Gyllene led from the first fence to the last, pulverising second-placed favourite Suny Bay by an incredible 25 lengths. The racing world had more than one reason to remember the National of 1997.

Tony said: 'I only live an hour from the course so I rang a friend and walked to the motorway to be collected. I actually played golf on the Sunday and had a fairly quiet weekend. I thought before the race that it was going to be a bit of an anti-climax. But when I arrived at Aintree again the crowds were fantastic. It was a great buzz, a different kind of feeling and could not have been better.

'I took it like any normal race. I know it was the Grand National but as soon as the tape went up I might as well have been at Sedgefield as at Aintree. I just took every fence as it came. I was in the lead by the first because I intended to make the running but I had not thought we would be quick enough. But as soon as we jumped the third I knew the horse was really taking to it and I wasn't going to disappoint.

'I was just a passenger, my horse was so good; all I had to do was steer him in the right direction. It was a dream ride and an unbelievable thrill to win. When I came up the straight and looked around and couldn't see anybody I found it hard to take in – I thought someone must appear from somewhere. It was a fantastic buzz; every bit as good being on the Monday, if not better.'

Michael Caulfield found it the most moving experience of his ten years in charge of the Jockeys' Association and he was amazed at the reaction of his members. 'Contrary to what people might think, the Anglo-Irish relationship was even better after what happened,' he said. 'The atmosphere of the whole weekend was absolutely incredible. The relationship between jockeys is amazing anyway, and it became even stronger.

'It was the most memorable sporting weekend I have ever been involved with. Everyone was at the same level. But above all they just wanted the race to be on; it had to take place; just had to take place. I've never known the jockeys to be in such good form despite all the hassle. The officials were just out of this world, the spirit was incredible. It would not have happened at Kempton, at Ascot, or even Cheltenham. It had to be Aintree. There was a sheer will to succeed and make it happen.

'The message from racing was crystal clear. We will not give in.'

5

The Police

THE bomb threats made by the IRA on Aintree Racecourse on Saturday 5 April were considered to be very real indeed. It was what could best be described as a state of emergency, as a result of which overall direction of the emergency was moved from police control at the racecourse to police headquarters at Canning Place, close to Liverpool's Pier Head in the city centre.

Charles Barnett and Peter Daresbury were the first of our team to leave Aintree and Charles asked me to stay with Judith Menier of Martell whilst she made an urgent rendezvous with a colleague close to the police canteen in the horsebox park. Judith and I waited there for what seemed an eternity. Not until some time later did Judith find out that it was Ian Harris, Martell's marketing director, who she was supposed to meet but, as it turned out, the rendezvous never took place.

Whilst we were waiting impatiently it became very clear that the racegoers were the really unlucky ones. I am a great admirer of the British police and none more so than the Merseyside force. I have never wanted to be a policeman but looking around their canteen I remember thinking how much better off they all were at that time than the racegoers standing out in the surrounding streets in what was becoming a singularly chilly April evening. At least the police could meet up in the comparative warmth with hot refreshments. This may seem a touch unfair because I guess none of these officers could look forward to too much sleep over the next day or so, however at least they were having a chance to put something warm inside them.

We had to abort our meeting and returned as quickly as we

could to the control point. Charles and Peter had already left and a vehicle would shortly arrive to collect Judith and me. We would also be joined by Roger Buffham, the Jockey Club's head of security, who would be collected later. I don't know what sort of journey Charles and Peter had, but if it was anything like ours it could at best be described as exhilarating and at worst terrifying. We were collected by an armed support vehicle, a converted Rover from the series before the current one. The driver seemed very young, his colleague looked a touch older and sat with an automatic weapon across his lap – which I understand was a Heckler & Koch 9mm semi-automatic – a weapon built to kill. The inside of the Rover was strange with various bulbous containers restricting seating space. This, I was informed, was where the guns were housed.

As we drove away I felt really guilty leaving all these people, none of whom had a clue what was happening. We had to drive down the Melling Road so Judith and I saw some familiar faces. 'When we clear the course congestion we'll put the light on,' said our driver. After crossing the Ormskirk Road which resembled a battlefield, we turned left opposite the Sefton Arms and then they put the light on, which to you and me means turning on the siren. I'll not forget the next ten minutes for as long as I live – it may have been less than ten minutes, but the journey to Pier Head from the racecourse in traffic normally takes me half an hour.

Although it was a Saturday afternoon and a lot of people would still have been glued to the BBC, there were plenty of cars around, and buses too. The drive was unbelievable, right foot to the boards all the way. One manoeuvre across a double red light and between two buses wouldn't have been out of place in a scene from *Bullit*. Judith doesn't remember it as she tells me she had her eyes closed for most of the journey. I love driving fast but this was something different and what amazed me was that our young driver relied almost entirely on calls from his colleague when we were approaching junctions. 'Moving car right', 'Lights about to change', 'Moving traffic left' were regular instructions. I wasn't sure we were really in that much of a hurry and to a certain extent felt this was a bit of a show put on for our benefit. When we arrived at police HQ both Judith and I disembarked with a great sense of relief. Sponsor-racecourse relationships aren't usually so dramatic.

Deep inside the police HQ the Aintree ops room was already up and running with the bank of phones ringing continuously. We were hustled into an ante room where we met up with Charles and Peter, who were already in discussion with senior officers. Our first task was to make some crucial phone calls and eventually we were offered a room with outside lines from where we could operate in private. Very soon Roger Buffham arrived from the course, presumably after a similarly enjoyable drive.

We needed to examine all the options with our crucial consideration being when the race could be run and under what conditions. Discussions had to take place with each and every trainer to see whether their horse would be able to take part in a rescheduled race, the British Horseracing Board to establish when the race could be run under the same conditions and without having to reopen entries, the betting industry, to establish the exact position in respect of ante post and day of the race bets, the BBC to see when a suitable slot was available and of course our sponsor Martell to see whether we had their support. Fortunately we had Judith with us so this part was easy.

Lord Daresbury was also anxious to establish the exact position in respect of Her Royal Highness The Princess Royal; would she be able and prepared to return for the race. If we weren't to be beaten by these mindless individuals such an endorsement would be completely invaluable. Another call Peter made was to Nicholas Soames to ensure that the Home Office should be in no doubt of our commitment to run the race as soon as possible. Nicholas Soames saw Michael Howard, the then Home Secretary, at 10 a.m. on Sunday to pass on the information and there seems little doubt that this action helped ensure that the National was run on Monday. So impressed were the Home Office with the fortitude of the Aintree team that it had been agreed that the Prime Minister John Major would attend.

Peter had also called his home in Daresbury to order us some refreshments which, I can assure you, came in very welcome an hour or two later. I can well remember some ham and cheese and pickle sandwiches as well as some cold drinks and Hula Hoops.

It's strange how, even in times of stress and crisis, one is able to remember the most insignificant things. Perhaps these are what bring us back to reality and help us keep our feet on the ground.

The last people Peter was to call were his team from Brunswick Public Relations, who represent Greenalls Group, of which Peter is Chief Executive, in the City. John Sunnucks and Kevin Byram were close by for the rest of the experience and proved invaluable confidants and advisors. Within half an hour they had arrived at the police headquarters, but thankfully for them by taxi.

Judith Menier was desperate to make contact with her team and colleagues. She was also beside herself with worry over the plight of her several hundred guests who had travelled to England and to Aintree from all over the world. Corporate hospitality is a vital part of this sponsorship and both Martell and parent company Seagram invite some of their major clients to what should be a truly spectacular day out. Her first call was to Martell's in-house security department. Their role is to see to the safety and well being of the Martell and Seagram executives and staff as well, of course, as their guests. Amazingly they were still in their office on the racecourse long after the evacuation had supposedly been completed, not, in fact, leaving until 11.20 p.m. Although somewhat foolhardy this was certainly a brave act on their part as it enabled a great many people to keep in contact using them as a focal point.

Charles had made contact with the British Horseracing Board's chief executive Tristram Ricketts to discuss race planning implications. Basically there appeared to be very few complications provided we could run the race within 48 hours. It was arranged that representatives of race planning would meet up with us at 8.30 the next morning at Peter's house.

We also contacted Johnny Weatherby, Peter's brother-in-law but more crucially in this context Chairman of Racing's Secretariat Weatherby's, who immediately agreed to take over the responsibility of contacting all connections to obtain their blessing and commitment to run their horses without which we would be wasting our time. Johnny was staying with Peter so we could touch base later on.

For my part, I had kept in regular contact with our team back at the course. Things there were as well as they could be although anger and frustration was growing. Locals were making their way home and there was still a hope in many eyes that cars could be removed that evening. This was very much a false hope as by then the police had announced that no cars or coaches would be permitted to leave the car parks until Sunday morning at the earliest.

I also maintained close contact with Joe McNally, who was back in his house on the Melling Road. Here Mark Popham and his Racenews team computers, printers *et al* had already set up a temporary press room which enabled us to keep in touch with the world's media, in particular to advise them of the latest decisions and advice from the police. This was great, but I had already decided that we would need to find a more suitable venue to be operational very first thing on Sunday morning. Phone calls completed, we were then invited to the police inner sanctum for an informal chat. It was in these circumstances that Charles delivered his 'We'll fight them on the beaches' speech which convinced the police that running the race this weekend was absolutely critical. I am sure that had the point not been so forcibly made the police would have been trying to persuade us to postpone indefinitely, or even cancel. The disappointment of owners and trainers and the loss of treasury tax and betting levy were understandably of little interest to them whereas the clearance of the site without incident and the safety of racegoers was.

When major events take place the police structure breaks into three levels of command. Gold, as the name suggests, heads the operation and once the event is under way plays a watching brief, unless of course there is an emergency. Silver is responsible for operation on site with Bronze working to Silver in specific areas on site (there were eight Bronze inspectors at Aintree).

Major towns and cities have crisis plans involving the police, other emergency services, the local authority and social services. These bodies would be called together by an emergency planning unit for any state of emergency such as an explosion, fire or plane or rail crash involving a large number of people. The IRA threat to the world's greatest race was one such situation.

Assistant Chief Constable Paul Stephenson was Gold Commander, aided by Chief Superintendent Paul Burrell, who had had first hand experience of Aintree as a previous Silver commander at the National. Paul Stephenson would in turn report through to his Chief Constable Sir James Sharples. At the course our main points of contact were Superintendent Ian Latimer, the Silver Commander, and his number two Chief Inspector Sue Wolfenden.

We attended the first of several meetings called by Gold Command. There were about 20 present, including representatives of the emergency planning unit, the council, the social services, and various emergency services. It became clear early on that there was still an underlying view that the race could not take place in the foreseeable future. We were able to convince the meeting that we would be ready and again we reinforced the importance of the race to the nation. At least it was agreed that the matter would be left open until the morning.

It was also clear that a lot had been happening since the commencement of the evacuation. Discussions took place on the availability of emergency accommodation centres, the need for warm bedding, plus the availability of food and drink. Transport was also a key issue and buses were to be sent to the course to take the beleaguered racegoers to these emergency centres. It really was the Blitz approach and something that however well you plan you are never really ready for.

We continually emphasised our concern for the racegoers, thousands of whom were still milling around outside the course. For my part this was all that really mattered at this time. Discussions on what would happen next were really secondary; we simply had to sort out our customers first. What we didn't know at this stage was what was happening out there on the ground and how the great British spirit was again responding in the face of adversity. The locals were opening their doors and people were using amazing initiatives to make their way home or back to their hotels. Nobody was going to be beaten. It was the same resilience that had achieved so much for our country in two World Wars.

Gold, via the police press office had called a press conference for later that evening and we decided that it should only be Charles who should talk on behalf of the racecourse and he would join Paul Stephenson to face the cameras and press corps. We had no idea who would be at the press conference, after all, we had been cocooned inside police HQ for some four hours. When we entered the briefing theatre it was good to see some familiar and sympathetic, friendly faces. I remember Julian Wilson being there as well as the team from BBC Radio 5 Live; several of the racing press had come and both the trade papers, the *Sporting Life* and the *Racing Post* were there. In addition there were loads of news reporters (not always so friendly) and various TV and radio crews as well as all the local media.

The press conference had always intended to be brief and the media seemed to accept this as reasonable under the circumstances. Paul Stephenson outlined the sequence of events and confirmed that two bomb threat calls had indeed been received at around 2.50 p.m. He also reiterated the fact that as no precise time or location had accompanied the calls that was the reason why it had been deemed necessary to evacuate the whole course, not just the grandstands, and why it was therefore imperative that no vehicles were permitted to leave until they too had undergone a thorough search. With more than 6,000 cars and coaches within the racecourse boundaries this was a mammoth task unlikely to be completed until well into Sunday. He ran through all the arrangements that were in hand for stranded racegoers and how regular statements would be issued to keep people informed. Radio Merseyside would be used as one of the catalysts for communication.

A host of questions followed and Mr Stephenson dealt with them firmly and fairly. There wasn't actually a lot he could add to his statement other than to reinforce the fact that public safety would be paramount and that after the Wilmslow bomb and the activities on the M6 earlier in the week this incident at Aintree was a major alert. Naturally the question was raised about the controlled explosions and whether or not this could now be deemed a hoax. The Assistant Chief Constable was adamant that this conclusion could not possibly be drawn until the site, including all vehicles, had been swept by the police search teams and thereby deemed totally safe.

The questions to Charles were naturally related to the racecourse and, in particular, when the great race might be run. As to the racecourse, it was known that fence damage had been caused by some over-enthusiastic evacuating racegoers, that a considerable amount of plastic running rail had been flattened to ease crowd movement, and there was inevitably a great deal of casual debris all over the running surface. It was rather difficult for Charles to answer this as he had not been back to Aintree since around 5 p.m. but he assured everyone as best he could.

* * * * *

Chief Superintendent Paul Burrell was relaxing at home; a rare chance for a man in the higher ranks of the Merseyside Police Force. Years of experience persuaded him to take the chance when he could; a Saturday afternoon, his wife out at the hairdressers and the Grand National, an event he had worked on for the last three years, about to start on the television. What better than to put his feet up and enjoy the spectacle from the living room of his Wirral home?

Chief Superintendent Burrell was on weekend cover for Gold Command, and briefly his thoughts flickered back to 1993, the year the race did not take place because of the faulty start. That April there were also genuine fears of activity from the Animal Liberation Front, an organisation sinister in its threats and always one to be carefully monitored during the three days of the Grand National meeting. 'I had gone to see the 1993 race with my wife, paid to get in and watched this horrific spectacle. I'd never seen a Grand National live before and it was the race that didn't start. By then I knew I would be Silver Commander in 1994 and I remember going home with my wife and almost putting my constabulary head in my hands and thinking: "Christ, how am I going to change the policing plans to cope?"

'Looking at the policing side it wasn't very focused, it was the old Lancashire County plan, it was a great day out for the bobbies. That incident of the non-start took us into a new era about protesters, about terrorists at a high profile event, and about things like were Martell going to withdraw sponsorship, was the Grand National viable, will Merseyside lose it, will the Aintree Racecourse Company suffer. That brought increasing pressure on the police to make it happen. For the next two years as Silver Commander with my team, we made it work.'

Chief Superintendent Burrell was as confident as a senior policeman will ever allow themselves to be. Two years before, there were again serious concerns about animal rights protesters disrupting the day, but he had stood in front of the BBC Television cameras and boldly told Desmond Lynam and the millions of television viewers: 'This race will go on.' This year, the first two days of the meeting had been staged without incident of note, and he could see from the television screen everything was going smoothly just a few miles away. No need for undue concern.

'I'll often go out and patrol the course but knowing how busy it was going to be I thought I would stay at home,' he said. 'I sat down in front of the television and saw Des Lynam and remembered being interviewed by him. It was getting close to the race and I thought I would have a can of lager. I went into the kitchen and thought, "No, I'm on call so I can't have a lager". So I put the kettle on, wandered back in and I thought someone had switched the programme. There were all these people spilling out and I thought this can't be happening, what is it? Then the serious overtones came out, that there had been a threat. I thought: "Oh shit". I actually started to reach for the phone and then the bleep went. Within 20 minutes I was upstairs at the police station in Gold Command.'

At the racecourse, the trouble for many of the senior police officers was only just beginning. Always vigilant, there was nothing they could do to counter two authenticated IRA bomb threats to an area 250 acres in size. No target point, but 60,000 excited racegoers waiting for the highlight of their day. An explosive device could be within their midst.

Inspector Mark Sutcliffe was the police search adviser that day, known as POLSA. In the event of warnings of trouble his task was to oversee the search team, to ensure any targeted or threatened area was clear of danger. If there was a bomb, he had to find it. 'I have a specific brief to search and give advice on security matters, with regard to IRA or whatever, and how it will affect a specific event, whether military, Aintree or anything else,' said Inspector Sutcliffe. 'The buildings are searched prior to the weekend and the actual course is searched. With royalty being present we check the buildings at a certain time to make sure nothing is in there. In previous years we haven't searched the whole lot because Aintree has never been a specific target. But this year there was royalty and some high-profile visitors.'

Inspector Sutcliffe co-ordinates the various teams, ensuring no area is left unchecked, no devices are concealed in places unthought of. His taskforce has the advantage of dogs to help them, of electronic equipment so sophisticated it is kept under wraps so no organisation will ever know of its capabilities. Their checks prior to the racing on Thursday, on Friday and again on Saturday had revealed nothing of alarm, but that was no reason to relax.

'To keep a place sterile is virtually impossible at somewhere like Aintree,' he said. 'The dogs are a back-up to the search teams; you would never put a dog in on its own as it can't tell you that a room is clean. It is a secondary device because only a person can say: "I've searched that room". We call it a rummage search; officers will touch things, look at things, look into any void or vacuum. We have all sorts of electronic devices we use as well, including the obvious ones such as X-rays, sound devices and mine detectors. There is also far more sophisticated equipment which we use.

'I could say with some certainty the buildings were all right unless somebody had brought something in on the day. If a device goes off and a member of the public gets injured it's bad publicity for the IRA, particularly with so many Irish people at the event, plus Americans and the kids. They don't want that happening.'

Despite the checking, double checking and more, Inspector Sutcliffe is not a man to leave anything to chance. As his team and the rest of the Merseyside police force remained vigilant to anything untoward happening that day, Inspector Sutcliffe decided to take up a position with maximum viewing. 'I was on top of the County Stand because I had a fear of mortar attack,' he said. 'If the IRA had staged a mortar attack, similar to that which they used on the airports, and at Downing Street, and it had landed on the track that would have disrupted the race. I had patrols, what we call mortar based, out and about looking at all the places.'

Inspector Sutcliffe thought he was in the best place to cover any eventuality, to react if needed, to ensure the safety of the crowd, the racehorses and the racing industry. However, he now has doubts. 'I put myself in a position where I could see the whole scene,' he said. 'Whether that was the best place for me or not I'm not sure because when I heard over the radio there was an alert I had to get from the top of the County Stand to the police communications room and to Superintendent Ian Latimer's side.'

It was the moment everyone with connections to Aintree and the Grand National had feared. Despite the meticulous planning, the frequent meetings starting soon after the previous year's event, the genuine and well-founded hope that the Provisional IRA would never target Aintree, an occasion packed full of Irish racing fans, the most alarming of scenarios was taking place before their disbelieving eyes.

Those in command had to weigh up the situation in seconds. An Irish caller, claiming to be from the IRA, had made two calls from a public phonebox. The man had used a known codeword, and stated there was a bomb on the course, but did not specify the exact location. There was royalty in the vicinity, 60,000 racegoers, politicians, hugely influential businessmen, children and families. The caller said the bomb would be detonated at 4 p.m. – little more than 70 minutes later.

Silver Command, under the control of Superintendent Ian Latimer and Chief Inspector Sue Wolfenden, did not take long to make their decision. They gave the order and Operation Aintree was under way, the biggest evacuation in the history of sport. The crowds, the guests, the press, the television crews and the VIPs had to be cleared from the course. Instantly.

Inspector Ken Laidler, due to retire just six months later, has had plenty of experience of the Grand National. He arrived on the Aintree scene in 1993 and one of the first jobs he was given was to find out what went wrong that year and to come up with a plan to prevent any repetition. 'We tried to alter it so we were more fluid and mobile,' said Inspector Laidler, head of the planning team. 'We thought we'd got everything just about perfect. For three years we gradually changed things and became more versatile. We introduced different radio channels and tried to look at everything that might happen, ranging from a plane crashing on the stands, to a bomb going off. We revised the evacuation plan. We treat bomb calls in different ways depending on the validity of the call. If someone rings up and says "There's a bomb at Aintree", we will take certain procedures and that would be the end of it. If there is a code word we obviously treat it more seriously and take other action.'

These two calls were regarded as the real thing; no question of taking risks. 'Because there was a codeword it was decided that Aintree would have to be evacuated,' added Inspector Laidler. 'It had to be treated seriously. The Princess Royal had to be got out and we had to start getting our procedures into place. The security staff and the police were told we would have to evacuate.

'Because the call was just to Aintree and not a location within the course, we would evacuate to the areas we knew would be safe. But because people who plant bombs sometimes do so in the vicinity of the call, we could be evacuating into danger. So if we stayed we were in danger and if we evacuated within the course we could be in danger. So it was decided we would have to evacuate completely.'

Inspector Sutcliffe remembers: 'I came down from the County Stand and ran through the crowds. It was a hell of a journey. I remember barging through and members of the public thought something really was going on. I was in full uniform and I didn't want to start a panic but I had to get through. The sight of me running made people realise it was for real.'

As Inspector Sutcliffe ran across the course, it struck him that a premonition had turned into reality. 'I'll try and draw an analogy,' he says. 'I recently went abroad on holiday and before I left I knew my car was going to break down, I just knew it, and it did. It was like that at Aintree; I knew something was going to happen, and it did. But you can't voice it. It's a bit like someone saying I'm not going on that flight, something's going to happen. Some people have the bottle to say they are not going to go.

'I ran over to Superintendent Latimer. I had a pager and I was also on radio communication when I heard the initial call. I saw the text of the messages, I looked at the wording, and I realised no one was safe.'

Gold Command, at Canning Place in the shadow of the Liver building, was detached from the emotions of Aintree – a deliberate policy to allow clear thinking, unaffected by the immediacy of the chaos, the confusion and, most importantly, the threat of a devastating explosion. Merseyside's most senior police officers could evaluate the situation untouched by the problems engulfing Silver and Bronze.

Chief Superintendent Burrell arrived at Canning Place after his shattered afternoon at home. 'I came into Gold and the system was humming nicely,' he said. 'The relationship is that the Assistant Chief Constable is the Gold commander and the Chief Superintendent provides Gold command when he is not there. I also act as his guide, calm him down, chivvy him up, advise him; like a mentor, but subservient to his view and quite rightly so.'

Chief Superintendent Burrell explained a small amount of the planning which preceded the Aintree crisis when he said: 'We had done a threat assessment and it was fairly substantial. It involves assessing all the available intelligence from a number of sources and then coming to a conclusion as to whether it is low, moderate or high. I think the assessment we had was probably moderate because there were lots of other events going on, though probably not as major as the Grand National. For example, the first year I did the Grand National I regarded as being high because they had just mortar-bombed Heathrow. I was doing helicopter fly-overs looking for the hot spots outside the course. That really was high threat.'

The planning and the risk assessment, however, had come to an end. The horrifying reality had to be considered, almost made worse by the uncertainty of whether or not it was actually true. They were under the most intense pressure; was there a bomb at Aintree? If there was, they had to clear everyone away before the clock ticked down to 4 p.m., the deadline according to the 10p call.

Matters were made worse when information reached the police commanders that, indeed, a car, coach or van, carrying a large explosive device, could already be within the confines of Aintree. It was critical that all members of the public were cleared from car and coach parks. Tensions could not have been higher.

Inspector Sutcliffe, with 17 years of policing experience behind him, remembers the impossibility of his task when he recalls: 'There was information to suggest that a large vehicular device could have been brought in. But we weren't given anywhere particular to search. Had the warning been: "There's a bomb in Number Seven stable" or whatever, we could have dealt with it. But 250 acres . . .

'I picked up a megaphone and actually went out and told people to get out because they weren't leaving. Once they heard the determination in people's voices, saying "You must leave, this is not an exercise", 90 per cent of people were as good as gold.'

Inspector Laidler, right in the thick of the action, recalls: 'The evacuation plan itself worked very well and everybody got to the exits very quickly. The stands were very fast to empty, although there were problems. One of the features of Aintree is that there are numerous bars and people enjoy drinking. When you are trying to deal with people who have had a lot to drink they are not as co-operative as they could be; some are downright argumentative.

'We managed to get everybody to the exits, although it was never planned to evacuate everybody from Aintree. We would move them from point A to point B, point C to point E, point G to point D, depending on the situation. We had the problem of evacuating everyone from everywhere so some of the exits weren't as spacious as they could have been. Because everyone was good natured and nobody panicked it went okay. If people had started running or horses had escaped that might have caused problems.

'We ended up with an evacuation that went very well but perhaps not as good as it could have been. The whole of the country has learned something from Aintree and various plans in various places are being revamped because of the problems that we had.'

Chief Superintendent Burrell, in the confines of Canning Place, says: 'In Gold we have a number of desks. There is the general police desk, there is the traffic policing desk, there's the fire service desk, the ambulance desk, there's the emergency services around the corner, there's the transportation of displaced persons, there's the logistical support, and we also have an intelligence desk. There was huge and constant intelligence even during the silent hours and that desk operated extremely well. If we needed further information we have other sources of intelligence we can plug into all over the place.'

While the well-rehearsed procedures for a major incident were put into place, more personal and confrontational problems surfaced for the Merseyside Police, problems that could never have been predicted even with the most thorough of planning.

'The operation took on a number of aspects,' said Chief Superintendent Burrell. 'Gold had to control what Silver was doing and Silver inevitably had their own views. Ian Latimer is very much like me and Sue Wolfenden; they were in charge, they were going to run that part – the evacuation, safety of people, property and then organising the bomb search. That was one hell of a task.

'Strictly speaking we should have evacuated Silver from the racecourse because we didn't know where the potential device was. The time was ticking away: was there a bomb, wasn't there a bomb. We should have got Ian out and effectively we told him to get out and he said: "No, I'm not doing this because I need to control here. If there's a risk, I'll take the risk. My staff can go but Sue and I need to be here."

'He was, in fact, correct. Had a bomb gone off he would have been incorrect. But that's the life of an operational bobby. You make decisions. He was right and he stayed there, but all the time we at Gold were pressurising him for information: "What's the situation, what's the crowd, what's the traffic like, what are the broader issues of what is happening there, at the railway station, the roads, pubs?" That's going on all the time.'

Evacuating the course, the largest exercise ever undertaken at a sporting event in the United Kingdom or, indeed, the world, was achieved with remarkable success. Despite the problems of a reluctant and sometimes disbelieving throng of racegoers, most of whom thought they would be back on the course within minutes to watch the spectacle they had paid for, the police managed to clear Aintree before 4 p.m. Despite that initial triumph, a credit to their operational planning, Gold and Silver Commands were only just beginning to kick-start their weekends.

Suddenly bigger issues starting to come into play. Although the police had achieved their first objective – clearing the course of people when they were told a bomb was about to explode – those evacuees had left without a moment's warning; when Operation Aintree was called, hats, bags, coats, umbrellas, mobile phones were left wherever they were sitting. Most significantly, thousands of cars were parked in the middle of Aintree, and there was no way they were going to be moved that night before being searched for explosive devices.

The search began immediately, and if anyone leaving the course, milling around outside, trying to find family and friends they had lost in the scrum, had any doubts about the seriousness of the situation, they were soon jogged unceremoniously to their senses when they heard explosions coming from inside the racetrack.

'There were three packages that were disrupted by the bomb disposal after the evacuation,' said Inspector Sutcliffe. 'The bomb disposal were by then on site and we asked a second unit to come because once one is deployed to a device you need another one to come in.

'Having evacuated the place I immediately started my plan to search Aintree from start to finish. Initially I had just the one team. A search team is made up of a team leader, and two or three pairs of searchers. I was dragged back from Aintree to come to Gold Command, which was a bit of a nuisance because I had things to do at the course. I came down with Major Chris Snaith from bomb disposal. We know each other quite well through previous exercises. We got a fast car, and it was fast. We went to Gold and everything was thrashed out of what they wanted, and we decided to keep the cars in Aintree overnight.'

That decision to leave all vehicles on the course until they could be searched the following morning caused some debate between the police officers. Some believed that since there had been no explosion up until 6 p.m. – well beyond what they term the 'soak time' – it would have been easier on Liverpool and the racegoers to allow the crowds back in to drive away. Gold Command, however, decided the risk was too great; if any single vehicle had contained an explosive device and it had detonated, injuring and possibly killing innocent civilians, the consequences would have been too much to bear.

Chief Superintendent Burrell says: 'The way it is supposed to work is that Silver has command of the incident on the ground, he will communicate his tactics to Gold and they will take on board the overall strategy and give appropriate advice and most certainly will feed them with resources if need be. Gold needs to be reassured and there's often a communication difficulty. We're seven miles away. We've got a few phone lines. How is Ian going to reassure Paul Stephenson, who knows that the Prime Minister and the Home Office have got a personal interest? How does he know what questions the PM is going to ask or the Home Secretary is going to ask? He needs to get all that information from Ian Latimer.

'Releasing the cars on Saturday night was considered. But with the nature of the threat we were dealing with when we were told there was a bomb on the racecourse, told it was going to go off and we didn't know where it was or if they were telling the truth about the time, we just had to be careful. Imagine how we have to think ahead to what we tell the Coroner's Court and the Judicial Inquiry if we get it wrong. We have to consider these things.

'Supposing we let the cars go at 6 p.m. and if one of them had been a car bomb that either hadn't gone off due to a defect in the fuse, or was timed to go off at 8 p.m. or 10 p.m. or midnight or the next day? Is it a defective bomb, is it a booby-trapped bomb so that when someone gets into their car it's going to go off and blow a lot of people up? And what's the maximum length of time before we can consider it safe? We liaised with our intelligence agency and we found the maximum length of time the IRA have ever manufactured a fuse, apart from the Brighton Hotel bomb, and we use that time as our earliest safe time.

'I can tell you that when we went through this conversation between us there was a huge temptation to say let them take the vehicles. We could see this looming problem overnight, over the weekend: "What the hell do we do with all these people?" I think it was the biggest thing since the War. Personally I was dreading it, thinking how the hell are we going to get this to work. We don't regret any decision we made, although we accept we could have done some things quicker.'

While Gold and Silver wrestled with their various problems, Inspector Sutcliffe concentrated on the biggest issue of all – finding any bombs within the perimeter of Aintree before the Grand National could even be thought of being run. 'We also initially had a secondary problem on the course that all the gas fires were lit in the catering areas, and we had to make a decision. We were still within the soak time and those buildings were not sterile. It wasn't safe but we had to make a decision to have them turned off because they would have caused a fire anyway.'

'I had to plan the whole search and I was up until the early hours doing it. I went back to get my papers, to brief my personnel on what I wanted, to get them all back on duty for 6 a.m. and I went back to HQ to plan my search.

'I remember my wife phoning because she had been watching the television and we had planned to go mountain climbing in North Wales the next day. She said "I suppose that's off, is it?" It was a pretty safe bet there.

'After the evacuation there was a bit of a lull, because everyone was out and the police areas had been searched and were sterile and I remember thinking then that this was history in the making and I actually voiced that to a couple of my colleagues. Standing nearby were a couple of people from Letheby and Christopher, the caterers, and one of them was in tears because of everything that had happened. I don't think my comments were going down too well.'

The perimeter of Aintree was patrolled all night by police officers, ensuring no one could gain access under the cover of darkness. Outside the fence, thousands of people were on the streets of Sefton and Liverpool, a logistical nightmare for the local authority, and a potential problem for the law.

Mounted police moving thousands of racegoers out of the course
and away from danger *(Bob Williams)*

The crowd leaving the course at Anchor Bridge had little room to manoeuvre
(Liverpool Daily Post and Echo)

National runners mingle with mounted police and shocked racegoers in the parade ring
(Liverpool Daily Post and Echo)

Early moments of the evacuation from the County Stand
enclosure and winners' enclosure area
(Stephen Shakeshaft, Liverpool Daily Post and Echo)

No more bets. Frustrated bookmakers make their way from the course
(Rob Judges)

An elderly racegoer is given a helping hand by racecourse stewards
(Liverpool Daily Post and Echo)

Racegoers look on as Robbie Supple surveys the scene
in the colours of the Martin Pipe Racing Club
(Liverpool Daily Post and Echo)

Line dancing or what? Letheby and Christopher staff, unsuitably dressed for the cold outside, pass the abandoned glass-fronted boxes *(Liverpool Daily Post and Echo)*

Change of restaurant. These racegoers still found time to enjoy their lunch in the Ormskirk Road

(Rob Judges)

England cricket captain Mike Atherton was one of the many famous faces left stranded
(Rob Judges)

John Prescott and racing journalist Julian Armfield await any news
(Rob Judges)

Photographer Bob Williams tries his hand as a mounted policeman,
after the successful evacuation of the racecourse

(Matthew Webb)

Mrs Teresa Chadwick *(centre, red and white dress)* with some of her Czechoslovakian refugees in her home on the Ormskirk Road

Eide Roche *(centre, front)* with some of the jockeys and racegoers to whom she opened her house after they were evacuated from the racecourse *(Pat Healy)*

'The next three days, I'll be quite straight, were one blur,' said Chief Superintendent Burrell. 'If you look at the Grand National as being a really major incident with displaced persons and overnight accommodation, public order could have been a problem. We started looking at the streets and I called in the Special Constabulary. They formed a small team and they took over the streets between Aintree racecourse and the City centre and they shouldn't be forgotten because they did a super job.

'That was the short term solution. Every area commander was called up and told to go to their own station and stand by there for instructions because we didn't know what the connotations would be. As we progressed we stood those down and called some in to handle things in Gold, so we then went on widespread alert.

We were now starting to plan the whole weekend in terms of logistics; who could we bring in, what was our overtime budget, could we pay people to come in. That's normal. We now had to look at the other side and think about the displaced persons. We went into the round table meeting held in the officers' mess to decide how we were going to handle it. That's when we started to realise we had other problems. The emergency planning people were very good but they couldn't actually tell us that they had blankets. They weren't too sure what the connotations were. It was all in place but it was the level to what was in place. We needed to put some controls in to actually make things happen because even policemen can get overwhelmed by the size of events.'

Chief Superintendent Burrell then attached an officer to various tasks including transport, who could work and provide cover, communications and the whole mass of other problems and potential problems that might have arisen in Liverpool that night.

'We had to set up communications with the local authority in order to open various centres,' said Inspector Laidler. 'First problem was we had to get in touch with the local authority; they then had to contact all their various heads of department who set up their evacuation reception procedures. They had to get in touch with their staff who could open the reception centres, then they had to contact the staff who staff the reception centres, the feeding, administration and so on. When they got to the reception centres they didn't know exactly what they were supposed to be doing. We had many thousands of people hanging about outside. It was decided that to get them away and the best place to send them initially would be the Albert Dock because it's a large area and we could get them there.

'The emergency planners had to call all the bus companies, who had to contact admin people, who had to get in touch with drivers and with mechanics, who had to make sure the buses were all ready to be on the road. They had to be called in from service, got to Aintree and then we had to decide the best way to send them because there were road blocks all around Aintree.

'We had all these systems to set up and all these homeless people. We had the people who were local but standing outside thinking it's another hoax bomb call and that they were going to get back inside and watch the race. We had to make sure everybody was told what was going on.

'I gave what I consider a simple request: we need the Fazakerley School open. If you're the caretaker of the school you turn up and want to know how much of the school is needed. He has no idea because we have just said open it. Did we mean the canteen, the classroom the gym? He tries to contact his boss, who contacts his boss, who tries to contact me so all these things are snarling things up.

'It was sometimes easier to send someone to walk across the field and talk than it was to try and get through on the radio. We will improve it but there is no system that is perfect when something goes seriously wrong. However much we plan there will always be problems.'

The planning and the problems went right through the night, and by Sunday morning the police were in a better position to communicate with the city, and the first message relayed was not to bother turning up to collect cars, as the search for explosives was still going on.

'There were problems there because some people just didn't believe us and turned up for their vehicles anyway,' said Chief Superintendent Burrell. 'There were problems with communicating with the people at the rest centres. We did actually have policemen there but we found it a problem communicating with them. We were discovering all sorts of problems with the subtleties of communicating very basic information, but bloody important if you're stranded from Peterborough and you're lying in some gymnasium with a great blanket over you; you haven't got your car, or your valuables, and your tablets and your inhalers and all that sort of thing. These were desperately important whereas in the bigger sphere of things in Gold we were perhaps a little bit slow to recognise that. But through interaction with other people we got it okay, although it certainly wasn't perfect.'

While Chief Superintendent Burrell and Inspector Laidler continued to wrestle with problems largely outside the course, the spotlight fell back on Inspector Sutcliffe, who went home to shower after completing his search plans but did not have time to sleep that Saturday night.

'I came back at 5.30 a.m. for a parade at 6 a.m., and by then I had the plans more or less in place,' he said. 'When I briefed the officers, about 100 of them plus their dogs, my objective was to search Aintree to make the place safe for people to take away their cars and for the place to function.

'No-one had mooted then whether or not there would be a race. I wasn't working to a deadline but I didn't dare tell the officers my objective was to have Aintree searched that first day so that people could go back to work. I didn't tell them because I didn't know whether they were going to be able to do it or not because I had never been faced with a situation with up to 6,000 vehicles and I just didn't know how long it would take. The briefing I gave was hopefully an inspirational one, where I made it clear it was not a day for people to be hanging round with hands in their pockets waiting for the next order. I told them it was a day to get on with it, they had all been trained and knew what was expected of them. If they came across a problem I told them to deal with it, not just refer it to me. They reacted magnificently.'

One of the first discoveries by Inspector Sutcliffe's team was a couple of vagrants who had somehow slept under cars in the night. 'We just could not work on 100 per cent security,' he said.

His officers then set about the task in hand. The first of these was to check all the vehicles so the racegoers, frustrated outside or waiting for information, could reclaim their cars and vans and at last drive home. Inspector Sutcliffe described the method of a vehicle search when he said: 'There is the eyesight test inside the car. If it looks like a genuine family car you are already feeling happier about it. You put a dog around it to give you extra confidence. You look underneath it, in the arches, if you can open the doors you have a look inside to make sure there's nothing untoward.

'Then we had the problem of identifying each car so we knew it had been searched, so we got sticky tape and put a large X on every windscreen. Each one takes several minutes depending on the size of it. You can also do a PNC – Police National Computer check – on any vehicle you are not happy with to tell if the vehicle has been stolen, its history. There were only a few cars that caused us a few question marks.

'We couldn't let cars out until we had finished because everyone would want them there and then and we could not explain to so many people why they had to wait. There were a couple of humanitarian issues with dogs in cars and we tried to search those first.

'By 1 p.m. it was getting to the point where the vehicles were sorted out and I was quite heartened by that. My main objective was to bring normality back to the people who had cars there. At least they could go home then. I wanted to cut the human misery.

'We had to make sure people coming to pick their cars up really were the owners. And we had to have a police officer with each person going to pick his car up because we had to make sure that no one was going to deposit something. There would have been nothing worse than had someone turned up and said their car had gone and the police had allowed it to be stolen. That would have been dreadful publicity.'

Despite the pressure, Inspector Sutcliffe and his team found one way to relieve some of the tension. 'We had a good repartee with Charlie Barnett,' he said. 'We had some Portakabin toilets by the office and you could lock them from the outside. Amongst all the people who came down to assist was a Special Chief Inspector. He turned up, pompous as anything with his stick and his braid and all his medals. He was all decked up and he was lording it here, there and everywhere and just getting on people's nerves and they locked him into one of these toilets. Charles was highly amused and this Special Chief Inspector did not want to lower his position by shouting for help so he said nothing. Forty-five minutes later Charlie came out and said: "Is he still in there?" He roared with laughter. Eventually someone turned the lock and this Special Chief Inspector walked out as though he'd been in there for two minutes. Charles loved the humour.'

Once that mammoth task with the vehicles had been completed, relieved racegoers were allowed to collect their cars and disappear. For Inspector Sutcliffe, the task had barely begun. 'Buildings were my second objective,' he said. 'It wasn't until mid-day Sunday I heard they were planning to run the race on Monday. They were asking if we could do it. It was then the stakes had been raised.

'As the cars were leaving I started on the buildings, the stables and the Tote – there was money still in there so we couldn't let anyone in. We started searching the buildings and the last leg of the search was the actual grounds themselves. We finished the whole of Aintree by nightfall. But I realised that to be absolutely certain we were going to have to search the whole thing again on the Monday and it paid off.'

Chief Superintendent Burrell recalls: 'We had a meeting on Sunday morning about whether we could run the race on Monday at 5 p.m. There was one gem from that meeting. We discussed in detail the ins and outs of who could come, what we could do with the remaining cars, what were the connotations if we got another threat. We had a really good, but tense meeting. Assistant Chief Constable Stephenson said: "Okay, are we agreed we are going to run it at 5 p.m.?" There was a general acquiescence and then he went round the table and asked if there were any problems. He came to Peter Daresbury.

'Peter said, absolutely deadpan, "There is one problem." Paul Stephenson asked him what it was.

'"Suny Bay won't like the going,"

'It was absolutely wonderful. It was him to a tee. I nearly fell off my chair. It was so English. This whole tense scenario; it was about policemen, bombing, the IRA. I thought that was a gem.'

The decision was taken and Aintree and the police prepared for the Monday race. Despite all their checks, the searches and the guarding of the course, no one was about to take any chances on the Monday. 'Before anyone was allowed in, everyone was searched,' said Inspector Sutcliffe. 'That included security people, it included everyone. I even wanted to search Specials, but we didn't in the end. Once word gets out that is happening, anyone thinking they will get a device in is put off. We publicise it so everyone knows. "If you're thinking of bringing anything in these are the risks you are taking. And if you try that we've got armed officers here."

'At 2 p.m. we were getting to the point where we were doing the last search on the helicopter landing point for the Prime Minister and also searching the racetrack – high visibility searching to reassure the public. There were certain things that were found: there was a heat measuring device that looked just like a detonator and that caused us a problem. There were other minor finds here and there which had to be dealt with, either by the bomb squad or by ourselves. We were ultra-cautious. Everything was suspect. That's human nature because the stakes were very high. 'At 2 p.m. I handed the course back to the Aintree Management and said "It's yours."'

Three hours until the delayed Grand National, 1997. The crowds were beginning to build up, determined not to miss out on the big race, the Princess Royal was returning, Prime Minister John Major was due to fly in for what he considered a vote-winning exercise in the final weeks before the General Election. The atmosphere was electric.

Then, a few minutes before the race was due to start, the almost inevitable disaster struck again. Two more warnings were received by the police, stating there was a bomb on the course. The tension in Gold Command was unbearable, and decisions had to be taken without delay. There was a small yet significant change in the warnings this time: the caller had named the areas where he said the bombs had been planted. Chief Superintendent Burrell recalls: 'We were all very tense because we knew we were taking a stand against terrorism, and we knew they would see it that way. What made it worse was the press were saying: "Stuff the IRA, the race goes on". And that was great for the British public but not so good for us.

'The Chief had now been in touch with the Home Secretary and the PM had been in touch. We got support to run the race at 5 p.m. And then we got the second two warnings and it got really tense. Even now it raises the hairs on the back of my neck. It was like a spectre "Hey, we're back". It was a horrible, horrible feeling. It was probably one of the tensest moments that I've experienced.

'Paul Stephenson was absolutely super. He went into almost an automatic mode. He sat down and went through possibility after possibility. 'Chief Constable Sharples was also involved. He was up there with Ian Latimer, lending support because Ian was making a judgement at the scene. I was with Paul and it was absolutely brilliant stuff, real war time commander stuff.'

'He made us think and rethink the decisions. Eventually he was content that he had exhausted every possibility, and we came to the view that the race would go ahead. We couldn't find any substantial reason for it not to.

'Over the weekend we had taken so many efforts to sterilise Aintree. We knew the way we had everything fixed we didn't have a vehicle bomb. Everyone had been searched on the way in, we knew as far as possible there was no bomb. If there had been one, it could only have been a small one. There was certainly no ton of semtex. And we knew that we had the crowds in such a way and after all our homework over the weekend that we ended up with a level of confidence that said there wasn't a bomb there. That was the professional judgement.'

Despite that confidence, no chances were taken. The police believed there was every chance their every move was being watched by a potential IRA bomber, concealed within the crowds at Aintree. They still could not be certain his finger was not resting on a detonator that would bring carnage to Aintree. Rather than ignore the possibility, which they believed would taunt the terrorists, the police staged a mini evacuation around the Parade Ring, making the IRA believe they were taking their threats with the utmost seriousness.

'Part of our strategic thinking was that if we were seen to react to it, that would give them the impression that we were listening and they were winning,' said Chief Superintendent Burrell. 'And then we could run the race and our job would be done.'

'It's similar to when we have a hostage situation, the rule is never stop negotiating because if you do then the hostage will be shot by the hostage taker. So we always show a reaction to what the hostage taker wants. If he says "I want a helicopter" we don't say no but explain that it will be difficult and keep him talking.

'We recognised it was a signal that we were reacting to what they said and therefore they didn't need to press any buttons if they could.'

Inspector Sutcliffe added: 'We got several warnings, focusing around the Paddock and the Winners' Enclosure areas. When Ian Latimer asked me I said there was nothing there. But to reassure him and the Chief Constable I searched again. I went with the search team and I wanted to be sure. I went to the Winners' Enclosure and we ripped it apart. I knew we wouldn't find anything and of course we didn't.

'That race was going to run and when it did I felt equally as elated as Charles Barnett did. All I got from it was the princely sum of £16.62 which is what I get for being on duty for a certain time without any refreshment. But our department put itself on the map, because we are always worried about budgets and about our existence. We were able to say: "This is what we've done for Merseyside Police, for Aintree, this is what we've done for the City of Liverpool."'

Chief Superintendent Burrell added: 'It was a huge victory for democracy and a small victory for the police force, but also for everyone else involved at Aintree.'

6

The Racegoers

IN the mid-'70s when local property developer Bill Davies held the reins at Aintree, raceday crowds had reached new lows. Aintree on Thursday and Friday resembled a morgue and the attendance on Grand National day was extremely average, well below the present day crowd attracted on the first day of the meeting.

Things started to improve under the management of Cyril Stein's Ladbrokes, although the nature of their contract restricted major expenditure on new facilities. So, even though some basic yet effective marketing and promotional techniques attracted thousands of new racegoers, the stands and structures were pretty antiquated and desperately in need of replacing. In many ways the racecourse was a disgrace but even this failed to take away the magic of the event, which was still very much part of our heritage. Had Ladbrokes been able to buy the course as they originally wished things would have been very different. Unfortunately Mr Davies was in no mood to sell at a price anywhere resembling a realistic figure. When ownership passed into the hands of the Jockey Club and subsequently Racecourse Holdings Trust, development of the course became a major priority. If we were to be proud to stage the world's greatest race we needed to provide a suitable stage.

Aintree now boasts three new grandstands and the management's objective is to continue to provide improved facilities. Those of us who have seen pre-television photographs of the massed crowds in front of the stands and on the embankment from the first fence down to Becher's Brook will understand why the National is recognised as the peoples' race.

National day is the only day when the course is opened on the other side of the Melling Road. This is known as the Steeplechase Enclosure and houses the Embankment and Canal Turn areas and there would be some 10,000 to 12,000 racegoers watching from various vantage points aided by giant screens. The remainder of Saturday's vast crowd is spread between the Tattersalls and County Enclosures within which there are a multitude of stands and facilities, some permanent and some temporary.

Over the last five or six years the crowds have grown quite dramatically and the embankment has been rigorously marketed and now starts to remind us of those old photographs. We now anticipate a three-day crowd of some 100,000, with around 60,000 on National day.

The County, Queen Mother and the new Aintree Stand house private boxes, reserved seating and some splendid roof viewing. The Glenlivet Stand offers reserved seating above some glass-fronted hospitality boxes and from the stable area right down to the Melling Road there are more hospitality units on several stories with some fabulous views overlooking the National start. Behind the grandstand there is a multitude of bars, restaurants, fast food outlets and shops as well as another massive chalet complex for corporate hospitality guests.

Hundreds and hundreds of staff are required to service such a complex including catering and bar staff, bookmakers and the very many Tote employees, ground staff and cleaners, contractors by the score, racecourse officials, Jockey Club officials, the television and radio crews, hundreds of press men and women, not to mention owners, trainers, jockeys and valets – a lot of people performing a lot of different and varied functions, all designed to serve the racegoers.

The thought of total evacuation has always been pretty far from our calculations even though all the procedures are in place. Our emergency procedures are regularly revised and discussed with all the relevant authorities, they are then circulated to key individuals before being fully rehearsed.

It is an extraordinary feeling to be on top of your job, to be close to your working colleagues, to be planning your next move when all of a sudden everything falls apart. Everything you have put in place is suddenly gone, the people you were close to dispersed in various directions, apparent confusion and chaos all around you and yet despite this emptiness you know exactly what is required of you.

As the vast crowd started to pour out of the stands and bars I was wondering how on earth we could begin to control any return and how long this might take. It reinforced my very first thoughts, that racing was over for the day.

Having done several interviews including Radio Merseyside and Radio 5 Live, the latter 'on the hoof', I walked with the huge yet amazingly calm crowd who were making there way between the Queen Mother and Glenlivet Stands. In a flash I was crossing the course near the finishing line and I'm not ashamed to admit there were times when I felt close to tears. I just could not imagine how we were all going to get through another 1993 scenario.

I called Charles Barnett to check on his whereabouts, which was still our original meeting place and he suggested I return there, which I did. It was weird walking back through the departing crowd into the almost empty main concourse area. Strangely enough, the thought of personal danger never entered my head for a second and I am convinced that this is how everyone reacts when their mind is completely focused on the job.

We stayed in our meeting place for some considerable time, although it only seemed like a few seconds. Suddenly Charles realised that if a device was to explode we were fast approaching the time that this might happen. Having spoken to the senior police officer on site we were told that now was the time that we simply had to evacuate and move clear of the grandstand areas. If I recall it correctly our group was made up of Charles, our Chairman Lord Daresbury, Ian Renton, Judith Menier from sponsors Martell Cognac, Bobby McAlpine and Richard Fildes, both Aintree directors, David Hillyard, Managing Director of Racecourse Holdings Trust (Aintree's parent company), Mark Savage from the Jockey Club, Owen Thomas, the BBC floor manager, and myself. The whole area behind the Grandstands was deserted apart from one or two groups of security staff, it was a very eerie and depressing sight and I remember thinking then that there was no way that we would have a hope in hell of returning everyone to their enclosures for many hours – the Martell Grand National was not going to take place on Saturday 5 April.

As I jogged along the back of the Queen Mother Stand I saw George Cowley, whose key role is to supervise our security staff who had the collective responsibility of organising a safe and orderly evacuation. 'This is the greatest moment of my career,' said George. At the time I could not believe that anyone could make such a bizarre comment but on reflection I understand what he meant. All the thankless hours spent rehearsing a total evacuation had paid off. For the time being our customers, the racegoers were safe, all public areas had been cleared swiftly and efficiently – George had done his job damn well.

As we scuttled across the course adjacent to the winning post the sight that met our eyes was very humbling: thousands of people everywhere, looking confused, anxious and in some cases angry. Police horses were shepherding large groups towards the designated safe areas and security men and women were tearing out lengths of plastic running rail to facilitate the flow. I felt so sorry for them all, particularly some of the Letheby and Christopher catering staff who were in their thin flimsy uniforms. It was clear that many, many people had left the stands and enclosures very unsuitably attired for what was to turn out to be many hours in the chilly Merseyside air.

In a way we were the lucky ones, because even though it was down to us to solve this nightmare, at least we would be in a building and have some clue as to what might be the likely sequence of events. Our main concern now had to be all these thousands of people spread around the vast acres of Aintree and shortly to be pushed out on to surrounding public highways to be a safe distance from grandstands and cars. There were more than 6,000 vehicles and as far as we or the police were to know any one of these could have housed a device planted by some sick-minded terrorist.

Bob Cox who, representing Racecourse Communications Limited, is responsible for the operation and management of the public address system at Aintree had the foresight to take with him a remote microphone. Before leaving his post in the broadcast office he had ensured that we could operate the public address from the centre of the course so we could at least attempt communication. What floored us, however, was when the majority of people were outside the course. Public address systems are designed to talk to people inside the course, all the speakers are therefore pointing inwards. After a very short time all our announcements were falling on very deaf ears indeed. History shows that all disasters or near disasters teach us vital lessons for the future. Maybe here is another one to be heeded by all courses or stadia. Speakers should be designed to cover 360 degrees so that they can reach out in any direction. I know it's easy to be wise after the event but our life would have been a lot easier if this had been the case at Aintree.

When our group reached the police control point situated inside the perimeter adjacent to the horsebox park I was given the task of preparing whatever announcements were deemed necessary and appropriate. I was able to reach both Bob Cox and Dave Bayes, who was IC for the police public address operation, via our radio communication network and feed to them the messages which we pumped out almost continuously. We asked people to remain calm whilst at the same time apologising for the enormous levels of inconvenience they were being caused. We begged patience and assured them that we were doing all we could to sort things out.

Before too long the police, realising the enormity of the security task and the length of time it would take to sweep the site, decided that racing would have to be abandoned for the day. Furthermore as all vehicles needed to be searched none would be permitted to leave the car parks until six o'clock at the earliest (very soon that was revised to Sunday). In the first instance (that is until the Sunday announcement was made) all people who had travelled to Aintree other than by car and coach were to be advised to make their way home as soon as possible. This was the text of the next series of announcements to which we added that racegoers should be sure to retain their raceday badges.

Aintree's marketing manager Joe McNally has a house on the

Melling Road which for the time being had been turned into a very temporary press centre, Mark Popham and his Racenews team having made their way there armed with computers and a printer. I was able to reach Joe by land line and he confirmed my very worst fears, the public address was inaudible, racegoers were unaware of our messages, and were becoming very frustrated and agitated as a consequence. It was only when the police helicopter arrived with loud speakers blaring that the news began to filter through.

The police infrastructure was shortly to remove control away from the officers on the ground to more senior officers at police headquarters in the city centre. It was decided that certain Aintree management should join the group at HQ whilst others should remain on the course. Charles Barnett, Peter Daresbury, Judith Menier and I would be taken into Liverpool. I left praying that things would start to improve for the thousands of racegoers – sadly they got a bloody sight worse.

* * * * *

Jan Lloyd is racecourse manager at Nottingham and for several years, like many in equivalent posts around the country, she has been drafted in on Grand National day to help bolster the Aintree staff and lend her expertise. But for a last-minute change of plan, Jan would not have been in Liverpool in 1997, but when her circumstances changed, she jumped at the chance of joining in such a spectacular occasion. 'I was given the job of looking after the parade of the 1st battalion, the Royal Ghurka Rifles,' she said. 'They were due to play behind the stands in the morning and on the course at around 3.25 p.m.'

The Royal Ghurka Rifles are a fairly conspicuous bunch of men in their full ceremonial uniforms, their 30 bagpipes and two bass drums, and their kukris hanging from their belts, even if the largest amongst them is barely 5ft 4in tall.

Jan went to meet up with them in the afternoon about 25 minutes before they were due to parade. 'I tried to get them up to the entrance to the course which was fairly difficult because there were such huge crowds. There was just myself and Joe McNally there to try and move them in the right direction. I was just chivvying them along when I heard the words *Operation Aintree* and I thought "shit" because I knew what was involved. I knew we would have to evacuate somewhere and then when I heard we had to leave all areas I just couldn't believe it.

'Joe at the time was chatting merrily away with the lady who brought the Ghurkas and hadn't heard any of this. I tapped him on the shoulder and said: "Joe, I think we might have a problem." At this point all of the stands started emptying out and of course everyone was heading towards the main entrance.

'I took them up to the corner near the start and thought we could take it from there. I was trying to push these Ghurkas through the huge crowd and we eventually got there and stood and waited for five or ten minutes before the police came and said we had to move. I tried to explain but they weren't having any of it; I waved my official badge but that made no difference, and by this time Joe had disappeared.

'I decided just to move them along about 100 yards and keep them all together. Most of them were completely bemused and we lost a couple of drummers which was a bit traumatic, but fortunately they turned up and that cheered us up a bit. We stood there a bit longer and began to realise just how serious it was because the police were pushing everyone on to the centre of the course. They told us we had to move. There I was with 33 Ghurkas and all their equipment, thinking "Oh, Christ, what do I do?"

'I thought I would just try and move them slowly, shuffle along, but by this stage there were so many thousands of people around. And because the Ghurkas look the way they do the crowd started to gather around and they wouldn't move . . . and all the time the police were shouting "Move on, move on."

'I thought the only way we could get the crowd to move was if we got the band to play, so I went to the Drum Major and asked if he could start up some music. They struck up a march and a huge cheer went up and we were allowed to set off. I started laughing because it must have been quite a sight, me at the front saying "please move", and being followed by 33 Ghurkas. We ended up in a line, me followed by the Ghurka band followed by thousands and thousands of people.'

Jan managed to march her charges towards the Melling Road, but as soon as they stopped the onlookers and the procession, enthralled by what they were seeing, began to close in again, encouraging new fears for their safety.

'A couple of the Ghurkas started to get really fractious and eventually one came up to me and said they desperately needed the toilet,' said Jan. 'Off they ran, with their weapons, to the portable loos on the Embankment. Fortunately we got them all back just as the police were getting more urgent about us clearing off the course. There was only one thing for it so we started them playing again. We went out of the Melling Road in a march with this huge crowd; it was like the pied piper.'

Just as it was for the thousands of racegoers, Jan's problems had only just started on leaving the course. There she was on the Melling Road, in charge of 33 Ghurkas considered a security risk being part of the military, and nowhere to go. Jan decided the safest place would actually be back on the course. This time she adopted a different approach. 'We marched them back again, only this time we were trying to do it quietly because so many people were following. We got to the entrance and tried to convince the police that they didn't really want these 33 Ghurkas wandering around Fazakerley in full uniform with their swords. They eventually ushered us back in and we got let in to a security compound which had all the first aid stuff in.

'These poor guys were absolutely freezing cold because they were only wearing very thin cotton tops. It was really windy and it got colder and colder and I was worried they were going to get pneumonia. They all sort of huddled together in a little group and I half expected them to dig a pit or something. I was beginning to feel really sorry for them and actually getting quite protective; I was clucking around them saying sorry and hoping they were all right. Eventually at about 6.30 p.m. we found a security hut, but it was all locked up. I got two or three comrades and we kicked the door down and pushed all these Ghurkas inside and there was a heater so that cheered them up.

'We were there for another hour and I managed to get back to police control and say: "Look, I've got to do something with these guys. I can't just leave them".

'They told me to take them up to the police catering area where they could be looked after, have a cup of tea, and sort out what we were going to do. This was about a quarter of a mile away and through goodness knows how many security areas. I managed to talk a couple of policemen into letting us through and then the Red Cross into lending us a couple of their little vans, which we packed them all into.

'I managed to get them all into the catering tent which was full by this stage with the police being briefed about what to do next. I went off to find the officer in charge to try and sort out a coach for them when someone from catering arrived and said there was a big problem and I had to return. I went all the way back and the woman who was serving said: "Who is going to pay for this lot?"

'I said: "Aintree will bloody well pay. Just feed them".

'I wanted to get them back to the coach which had all their military ID but there was no way. So I had to arrange somewhere for them to stay overnight, and it couldn't just be a hotel because they were a security risk. We spent two hours ringing round every military place; the police were radioing central office to see if any of their stations had spare beds.

'I was ringing up these military bases and they must have thought I was mad. One woman actually put the phone down after I told her I had 33 Ghurkas with me who needed a bed. Eventually we managed to get Chester Barracks to agree because they had enough room. It was then just a question of getting them there. I had to order a coach and then talk the police into letting them through their roadblocks. That must have taken at least another two hours.

'All they kept saying to me after all this was that I made "Good Ghurka. Honorary Ghurka. I hadn't deserted my post" because everyone else had left by this stage. It must have been 12.15 a.m. by the time I eventually put the last Ghurka on the coach and waved goodbye to them.'

Jan, unfortunately, was unable to return for the race on Monday. 'I had to drive home because there was racing at Nottingham on the Tuesday. I was really upset because a few minutes after I left the Ghurkas rang the course and said they were still in the area, did we want them to return. It was such a shame to miss them.'

* * * * *

Grand National day had started off in a singularly happy fashion for the Duke of Devonshire. After enjoying a fabulous lunch with the Princess Royal, he had watched her unveil the bust of Peter O'Sullevan, sculpted by Angela Conner, and commissioned for the course by the Duke himself.

'Then came the bomb warning,' he said. 'I was faced with one immediate problem. I had travelled to the course with Angela and had become separated from her. Luckily we met in the milling throng after we had both crossed the Melling Road on at least eight occasions.

'There followed an extraordinary piece of good fortune. I ran into the High Sheriff of Merseyside and her husband, whose car was outside the official car park since they had been looking after the Princess Royal. Mr and Mrs Grundy were kind enough to ask Angela and me to their home for tea, some five miles away. During tea Mrs Grundy apologised that she could not offer to put us up, as their house was full with their family. However, she suggested that she and her husband would be only too pleased to drive us back the 60 miles to Chatsworth. This astonishing offer we were more than delighted to accept. All I could offer in return was dinner at Chatsworth before they returned home again.

'This fantastically kind gesture annoyed my friends greatly, as many had expected me to be stuck away from home when in fact I was comfortably back in time for dinner. My driver was looked after by Lord Daresbury's driver, who very kindly arranged for him to stay in a comfortable local hotel until the car was released from the car park.

'My outstanding recollection of the whole day was the astonishing good humour of the crowd, who had been put to great inconvenience and disappointment, but who had treated it all so well. I was most struck by the generosity of those living near the course who so readily offered accommodation to those who were stranded. Indeed it showed the British public at their very best.'

* * * * * *

Tim Watson has been a television director for 25 years and in the last five has run his own company, called Reel TV. 'We are an independent facilities company providing hardware, cameramen, kit and equipment at horseracing,' he said. 'I was working on that day not as a director but as a supplier of equipment to Racetech, who mastermind the coverage for stewards. Specifically I was based down at the Canal Turn, where there was a big screen. We were providing radio links to get pictures back from the main grandstand and I was up on the top of a scaffold tower when the alarm went off. Everybody thought it wouldn't affect us because we were so far away; there wouldn't be any need to evacuate.

'Because I had the responsibility of providing the signals back from the grandstand we knew the Aintree evacuation procedure and the big screens were very important for that; they had to have messages on saying things like *Stay Where You Are* or *Please Leave*.

'I went to a police inspector and said: "Do we need to put an evacuation message on the screen?" She said: "No, no, no, it's miles away and we are perfectly okay". Just after that she came running up to me and said: "Yes you do, we've all got to evacuate". We all thought how bloody silly.'

As the crowds poured into the middle of the course, Tim stayed where he was with some other television crews from the BBC and horseracing specialists SIS. He then went and sat inside the structure holding the giant screen. 'We were all well accredited with arm bands and so on so we weren't getting hassled by the police,' he said. 'After about half an hour Special Branch arrived and tapped on the window and told us we had to go as well.

'We switched off all the mains and all the technical kit. I locked my car and I started walking up the field. I thought we would all be allowed back in after 15 minutes or so, but fortunately I had taken some extra clothes just in case. We started meandering up towards the Melling Road and suddenly I realised that everybody seemed to be exiting over this tiny bridge.

'Some of us commented that it looked as if it could turn into another Hillsborough situation, all these people being shoved in, police horses around and a helicopter overhead. I couldn't see how people could get away quick enough and there was the potential of being crushed.

'Anyway we hung back. I didn't want to go across because I knew as soon as I did they could seal the bloody place off and I didn't want to leave my expensive equipment. After a while there was just a group of us left, including some photographers. I was absolutely staggered when an announcement came from the helicopter that no one would be allowed that night back to their cars. I said to one of these press guys, "watch this, now you'll get your picture. There will be a bloody stampede here. People won't accept that, won't accept that they are going to have to leave their cars and won't be able to get back to them tonight."

'With that, there must have been about 2,000 people came rushing back. Trying to push through and they had thrown this police cordon across this bridge to stop anyone coming back in. Fortunately I and about five of the press photographers were the right side of the bridge. I thought, bloody hell, I'm getting out of here.

'I had noticed there was this enormous coach park in the middle of the course, there must have been 250 in there parked about four wide. I had seen a couple of coach drivers who were still there and I thought it would be a good place to go and seek a bit of shelter because by now it was cold, it was wet, it was really very unpleasant.

'So I slipped back and walked between two of these coaches and I saw a group of about five drivers on one of them. I tapped on the door and said: "Room for a little one?" and they said come on in. I don't know if they assumed I was a coach driver or what. I asked: "How come you guys are still here?" and one of them said the police had turned a blind eye because they thought they might need some coaches later to take people away.

'We were in this nice coach and it was centrally heated and air conditioned. It was raining outside and I said this is jolly nice. I asked them to put the radio on and we heard stories of people in Liverpool being thrown off trains and people fighting to get on transport. I was saying how lucky we were. Then about three photographers came along and asked if they could come on the coach as well. They agreed – the more the merrier. We sat there talking, it became dark and at about 9 p.m. one of these coach drivers said: "What about some food? Is anyone getting hungry?"

'I said: "Where are you going to get food from?"

'He turned out to be an ex-policeman from Glasgow and he either had the handshake or he had the right tie and he said: "I'm going to go and get some fish and chips."

'I said: "Once you go over that bridge, you will not be allowed back in."

'"You want a bet?" And he disappeared. That was that, we thought. We will never see him again. Half an hour later he arrived back in a police Land Rover. He'd got out through the police cordon and he'd got back with a box full, not of fish and chips because they had run out, but sausage and chips and some cold cans of drink.

'I was getting to know the photographers and one of them told me how earlier on he was over near some toilets inside the course and one of the policemen had got off his horse and asked the photographer to hold it while he went into the loo. The officer came out and the photographer climbed up on this horse and he put the policeman's plume on.

'By now they had set up this operation where they were patrolling the grounds with these very strong search lights and I said we should keep our heads down, and that was agreed. I was all for dropping off to sleep when round about midnight one of the drivers said: "Would you like some champagne?"

'I said: "Where the hell are you going to get that from?"

'What I hadn't realised were all these coaches were full of food for return journeys. So some of the drivers got off the coach. I said: "Don't do it lads. If you move the next thing you know there will be a bloody police dog biting your arse."

'They started lifting up the side doors of the coaches and they came back and there was champagne, chocolate eclairs, there were chicken legs, duck breast, Beck's beer. It was wonderful. We were having this orgy of food at one in the morning.

'Round about 3 a.m., the coach light was turned on and somebody must have spotted it because the next thing we knew this bloody Land Rover arrived. The police came on and said: "Right, you lot have got to go."

'We asked where the hell we were going to go at this time of night, that we were better off staying. We were, of course, terribly reluctant to leave. Then somehow the ex-policeman managed to swing it because we had all piled off, we'd grabbed everything we had, and they suddenly said: "Right, everybody back on". We all climbed back on board and were enormously relieved; the police drove away and we actually got some sleep until about 6 a.m.

'We woke up and the police had arrived again – they wanted to get rid of six coaches immediately. An officer said: "Right, we're going to search the coaches, make sure they are clear and you can go. Get the hell out of here."

'He looked at me and said: "Which is your coach?"

'"Er, I'm not actually a coach driver. I'm a television director."'

'He said: "Well what the hell are you doing here?"

'I went with one driver who was going to a hotel just off the M6, where his passengers were due to be. As we drove out we started seeing the sights; the left luggage, the handbags lying around. We just thought it was unreal. We drove out in convoy, six coaches. The TV stations were just setting up their satellite links outside the main gate.

'We arrived at the hotel about 30 miles away and the manager offered us breakfast – our third meal since the evacuation. I then phoned my colleagues, went to meet them at another hotel and got there just in time for lunch!

'It was an incredible night. We had stayed in the middle of Aintree in relative luxury, probably the only people there. I must have had one of the most delightful weekends of anyone.'

* * * * *

Keith Elliott is a tipster the bookmakers fear; the successful Winning Line is where his information on sports betting is devoured by eager punters. His knowledge of golf is particularly feared, but the former university lecturer is also an expert on football, rugby league and can spot a bookie's howler at a hundred paces. Politics is another area where his expertise has been put to huge financial gain, and the racing side of Winning Line uses Lester Piggott's expert knowledge to good use.

Keith also works for BBC Radio Merseyside as their racing correspondent, and he has a programme every Friday night from 9.30 to 10 p.m. and on National day he broadcasts live from Aintree. It is one of the year's highlights for the Liverpudlian. 'It is the day of the year when the eyes of the world focus on our city and our race,' he says. 'To celebrate I send my wife a bouquet, make sure I give my lads a couple of quid for a bet and off I go.

'This year was especially exciting as I was guest of the Winning Line, owners of General Wolfe, one of the fancied horses. I was in their posh box in the main stand an hour or so before I would go upstairs where I had set myself up with my binoculars and gear to start broadcasting when the alarm first sounded. A guy came in and it was the usual thing at the time, me thinking there is no point in leaving. Then he virtually took the glass out of my hand, very pleasantly. I thought there was no point in rushing to get my stuff from upstairs because we would all be back fairly soon, probably within an hour. On the way out from the stand I literally bumped into John Prescott, who I hadn't seen since the Wirral South by-election where we had done a broadcast, and a quick interview was arranged. The atmosphere was still buoyant.

'However, as we moved on to the road I began to realise that perhaps the race just might be abandoned, not just put back. Then the news of the cancellation came and Roger Hughes, sports editor of BBC Radio Merseyside, and I decided to go straight back to our studios in Paradise Street as my car was parked nearby in a side road. I never, ever park on the course so I had a fast exit into town.

'There was disappointment and sadness, but the real significance of what was unfolding had still not dawned on me. I was still 125 per cent convinced that it was a hoax, it didn't make any sense to me it could be anything other than that. We drove to the studios in Paradise Street and I wondered what I would say as

I knew that I would be asked to sum up what happened.

'In the studio the atmosphere was electric – a special extra programme had been arranged with the station boss Mick Ord producing it. Slowly, I realised that this was not really a racing crisis, it was a refugee crisis. It soon became apparent that was the real problem.

'The phones in the studios never stopped as listeners, many of whom I knew, rang in offering to put people up for the night and the racing refugees started arriving at the studios. The programme was live radio at its very best as the nature of the unfolding drama hit us all. I remember interviewing Barry Oldham, the Aintree farrier and a personal friend of mine, on his mobile phone before Willie Carson took the phone to tell us in understandably agitated tones that the horses had not been watered and there was going to be trouble soon if the situation continued. That was cracking good radio because it got across to the listeners just how restless the trainers were getting. Then I also heard Jenny Pitman's comments, and I cried in the studio as she summed up what everyone felt in a few sentences.

'In between those live broadcasts I ferried some of the refugees in to the studio to tell their story and to put them in touch with the people who had offered help. The people often had no money or anything. I knew the generosity of Liverpudlians was world class and slowly I realised that as a result of the day that generosity would be known throughout the country, throughout the world.

'So after the special programme, as I reflected later, on a day I will never forget, my final emotion was one of intense pride. I have always been proud of Liverpool and its people as a Scouse lad myself, I have always been proud of BBC Radio Merseyside, yet never as much as I was on the evening of 5 April, 1997. It was really uplifting.'

Keith has a couple of irksome memories from the weekend: 'This year, of course, I had to buy my wife two lots of flowers in three days, which was a bit much!' he said. 'Also, the disappointing thing for me was my selection for the race was Suny Bay and my dual forecast was Suny Bay and Lord Gyllene, which I had backed with The Tote on the Saturday. I then forgot all about that and of course the Tote therefore treated that bet as void, so I just got my fiver back, costing me the best part of £400.'

*   *   *   *   *

The Tote has good reason to prepare well for the Grand National; it is one of their biggest operations of the year. More than 60,000 racegoers on the course, almost without exception wanting to have a flutter on the outcome. For those who cannot face the rough and tumble of the bookies, the Tote is the relatively hassle-free alternative with their cash betting shops, their kiosks and cash pool outlets and, of course, the luxury of the credit account holders.

Joe Scanlon, managing director of the Tote Bookmakers, was inside one of the two betting shops and unable to hear the public address system. 'Someone banged on the door,' he said. 'They shouted "Bomb alert, clear the course." We carried on taking bets. Eventually a police inspector visited and insisted that everyone must leave.

'Joe Toner, the general manager of the on-course bookmakers, and I decided that we should stay and cash up the money. It took ages to sink in that everyone had to leave. We were waiting for 4 p.m. when the bomb would be due to go off. We were getting nervous and John Lyons, who worked for UXB after the war, said: "Well boys, the best thing now is if I go and make us a cup of tea."

'"Are you sure?"

'"We are in a wooden building, everything goes up and comes down on top of you. We are safe in a wooden building, unlike concrete."'

Joe Toner recalls: 'Security guards were screaming for us to leave, but the shop would have been vulnerable. Four other managers stayed with us and we pulled the shutters and stayed in the shop to cash up. We were there until 7 p.m. and we saw an irate policeman who couldn't believe we were still on the course. I had a rucksack with a great deal of money in it!'

Joe Scanlon continued: 'We then went to our other betting shop, near the Parade Ring, and the police and security were amazed again. That shop had been abandoned so we insisted we took the money out of the bulging safe. But we couldn't open it as they had packed it so tight and it was a digital safe with a time lock and I couldn't get the code to work. A policeman asked me: "Are you sure you chaps are with the Tote?" Joe said to me: "Come on fingers, you can do better that this." We put about £26,000 into another bag, left the course and walked down the main road looking for our staff. It was so eerie when we left. We walked past the jockeys' changing rooms and it was like the end of the world.

'We needed to pick up our red-coated staff and we walked all the way to the M57 looking for them. I rang a friend in Manchester and we got the last 12 rooms in the Hilton. He also hired us a mini-bus and we stopped off on the way and bought everyone shaving gear and toothbrushes.

'But we still had all this money with us and we didn't know what to do with it. In the end my friend took it home and put it under his baby son's bed, where it was guarded by his two rottweilers who adore the baby and wouldn't let anyone near him. That money was safer than the Bank of England.'

There was one twist when the race was run on the Monday which made all the Tote efforts worthwhile. A young mother walked up to a kiosk to claim a £1 refund, her stake in the Saturday placepot which she believed had been cancelled because only three races were run. But Rob Hartnett, the Tote's public relations manager, said: 'There was actually a placepot dividend. The mum with her two kids came to claim her £1 and she received £600-plus. The girl from our staff said she literally danced away from the window in joy. She walked away with a holiday!'

* * * * *

Letheby and Christopher have a function almost as important as the Tote – they are the specialist events company which has to provide food throughout the meeting, servicing the many bars, restaurants, chalets, marquees and private rooms.

'When the evacuation was broadcast we put our plan into

operation,' said Tony Roestenberg, the company's chief executive. 'After being caught in the mayhem on the M6 on Thursday I called a meeting of my managers to formulate a plan in the event of similar disruption. When the balloon really did go up, we were able to swing into action straight away.

'The Melling Road gate was our meeting point, for the staff and for them to deposit takings which we could then secure in our Portakabin. One of our problems was that our staff were in their working clothes and would very soon be getting very cold and hungry. They had left all their possessions behind, including their money and car keys.

'We moved them down to the local Asda store where we had made arrangements to feed them. This we did, and I might say, on the house, as Asda insisted on the food and drink being supplied with their compliments.

'We then had to think about getting our staff home, or at least into accommodation. We gave everyone some cash, and some ended up in local houses, some at the stable lads' hostel at Haydock Park, courtesy of Richard Thomas, and some at local hotels where we were lucky enough to find the rooms. All in all we managed to find beds for 300 staff who were not previously accommodated.'

The police allowed Tony back on site to his Portakabin, where he remained until midnight before going to stay with friends nearby. During this time he was able to keep in constant telephone contact with his regional director Karin Waring, who was at Haydock Park.

During the evening Andrew Tulloch was putting together his task force to tour and secure the whole site. 'Aintree wanted an L&C representative as we had a particular problem with water boilers which could easily explode, and if Calor Gas supplies were not switched off there was serious risk. We would not need to worry about an IRA bomb,' added Tony.

'Also we knew that there would still be takings which would have to be collected which our staff had been unable to bring out with them. I asked for a volunteer and at least 100 hands went up. I decided that Ronnie Phillips, our liquor control manager for the north west, had to be the man because of his intimate knowledge of the site.' For his magnificent efforts over the weekend Ronnie

Phillips earned the employee of the month award, which was presented at a lunch held for management and staff at Ascot racecourse.

At around 2 p.m. on Sunday, Tony had a call from David Hillyard to say there were a lot of hungry people on site. 'He told me that he was talking about meals for 1,000 and as amongst the hungriest were the police and security personnel we were allowed to bring 200 staff into the compound to handle the operation. The food was prepared and brought in from Haydock and we fed everyone in the police canteen.

'Later on Sunday, I was allowed to tour our facilities with police officers to assess what we would be able to do on Monday. I analysed each area and built up a plan in my mind. I then met with senior managers and we finalised our plan, which included clearing tons of food and gallons of drink which had been left by the racegoers, and to see what sort of fare we could provide the next day.

'We were able to bring around 1,000 staff, who were all needed as it was not until 11.30 on Monday that we could get in to start clearing up and preparing for two o'clock when the gates were due to open. In the final analysis we opened every bar in public areas, and in the Queen Mother and County Stands and we provided sandwiches and snacks and a full catering service to private boxes. The only areas that remained untouched and closed to the public were all temporary facilities such as marquees and chalets.

'I was very, very proud of all our people, it was a magnificent team effort. The atmosphere was terrific and everyone remained cheerful and friendly. There was a real bulldog spirit in the air, a determination to get the show on the road and not to be beaten.'

*   *   *   *   *

Andrew Dudley and his wife were pondering last January what to buy her grandfather for his 80th birthday when the thought struck them about a story he had told over the years.

John Herring had been to the Grand National just once before; in 1947, the same year Peter O'Sullevan's first commentary on the race was broadcast to the nation. That year, John had obtained a special ticket in the stands and had stood around for a while, taking in the atmosphere, when just before the first race he wandered down to the rails to put on an extra bet. On his return, the stand was so full the police would not allow him to take his place amongst the swollen crowds and with the fog so dense that day he never saw the 100-1 outsider Caughoo hack up for a remarkable victory.

Andrew and Louise thought they would make amends for that in 1997 and he, his wife's mother Wendy, and John and his wife Alice set off at 5.30 a.m. from their Stratford-upon-Avon homes and, with John being disabled, parked in the central car park close to the stands.

It was turning out to be a marvellous day. Louise's uncle John Spearing is himself a trainer and arranged for John to visit the weighing room in the build-up to the action. The group then found themselves an excellent vantage point in the County Stand and John won £120 on the first race and Louise £45 on the second.

Wendy and Alice decided to wander off for a few minutes before settling down for the big race. 'You could feel the excitement building up,' said Andrew, 'then, all of a sudden, the words *Operation Aintree* came over the public address system. You could tell it was quite serious as stewards and police were moving very quickly to what were obviously pre-designated places. Almost immediately we were told to leave the stands.

'We were obviously very concerned about Wendy and Alice and we tried to wait for them to come back. However, a policeman came up to us and said that we must leave immediately. We decided the best thing was to head for the car in the centre of the course as they would know where it is. But as soon as we got near the car park we were told none of the cars were safe and we must head out of the course. We made our way out, still convinced we would spot them because Wendy was wearing a very bright turquoise coat.

'Once out of the course we assumed we would be going back fairly shortly. We waited for some time looking for them as all the people came out but never saw them. We guessed that they had been sent out from the other side of the stands and decided to walk all the way around the outside roads.

'We asked a number of police what we should do about lost relatives, but they were understandably concentrating on the alert and did not know what to suggest. We carried on walking round past the front of the stands and along the main road until we reached a Pizza Hut.

'By this time John was very tired and we thought it best to rest there for a while. I decided that the only way they might be able to contact us was via a relative so we phoned Louise's Aunt Beryl, who became control point number one.

'I then left Louise and John sitting on a wall outside Pizza Hut and walked right the way round to the other side of the course. There were a number of buses parked on the road and I asked a local policeman what to do about lost relatives. He said that everybody was being bussed to Albert Docks where they should be able to meet up. I had to walk all the way back round again to meet up with Louise and John.'

The trio, becoming more and more concerned about their lost family, caught the bus into the docks, but there was still no sign. 'When we got there the main priority was to get people settled for the night,' says Andrew. 'The officials could only suggest that we go to one of the sports halls and, hopefully, we might meet up with them. By then it was 8 p.m. and dark and so I thought it would be best if we found some shelter for the night. I phoned control point number one but Beryl had still not heard from the other two.

'Up until that point we had fully expected to find Wendy and Alice and now we were becoming quite concerned, in fact, bewildered. Even then, I remember the bus driver cheered us up a bit as he gave us a guided tour of all the sites of Liverpool on the way to the sports centre.'

The worried trio were taken to a Methodist Church hall, only a few yards away from where they had originally caught the bus, to register before going on to the sports centre. Andrew said: 'We walked into the hall and I made my way straight to a kindly gentleman who was making cups of tea and asked him where I should register. He looked completely bemused and said: "Sorry, I have no idea – I am only making cups of tea". It turned out that the man and his wife were to be our hosts and saviours for the evening.

'I think we were in a state of shock. From having been wandering around aimlessly trying to find Wendy and Alice, all of a sudden we were in a hall where there was warmth, food, drink and organisation. Within minutes three separate sets of people offered us a bed for the night. To be honest we could not take it in, and initially refused because we still wanted to find Wendy and Alice. In the end, though, we accepted a bed from Des and June Roberts of Aintree.

'They finished serving cups of tea and sandwiches and took us back to their house. I remember they were very apologetic as they only had two beds and that one person would have to sleep on the floor. Believe me, to us the thought of just a roof over our heads for the night was paradise.

'As soon as we got there we reported in to control point number one to say we had definitely landed on our feet, that granddad would have a bed for the night and that we were settled with some very nice people. Des poured me a large scotch which did me a power of good.

'At about 11 p.m. the phone rang, and it was Wendy. The first thing she said was: "How have you lot ended up in a lovely house?" They were at the Everton Sports Centre with a chair and a blanket whereas we had beds.

'Without hesitation Des and June immediately offered to take me over to the Sports Centre to collect Wendy and Alice. Des has a serious heart condition and had been working for hours providing food and drink for people, but despite this he was still happy to set off late at night so that our family could be together. June was worried that she had not got enough beds for everyone, but we were delighted just to be together. I will never forget their generosity.

'Once we were all together we couldn't stop talking about our experiences. Apparently Wendy and Alice had managed to get to the car and waited there for about ten minutes before the police said they must move away. They were sent to the south of the course, to the bottom of the Melling Road, and waited in one place hoping that we might find them.

'In fact they had been standing by a hedge only 100 yards from the house where we were. In the end they went to Albert Docks and were sent to the Everton Sports Centre, where the manager was brilliant. They were particularly worried because John has a heart condition and his tablets were in the car. The manager let them use the phone and in the end she got through to control point number one.'

The following morning, after breakfast, the new-found friends strolled down to the local paper shop. 'On the way people we had seen at the Methodist hall the night before were waving at us,' says Andrew. 'They could see that we had found Wendy and Alice and they were genuinely pleased to know that we were safe.

'At about 11 a.m. it came on the Teletext that we should report to a local sports centre. Des took me up there but it turned out the police were still searching the course and that it would probably be mid to late afternoon before we would be able to get our cars.

'Des and June immediately said that we should stay for lunch, but they were very embarrassed that they did not have enough food for seven people. So we set off to Safeway, bought a chicken and all sat down to a sumptuous Sunday meal.

'By now John was getting worried that he had not taken his heart pills, which were still in the car, so I went up to the course. The local police were wonderful, although they were having a difficult time dealing with some awkward Irish people who could not understand why they could not go and collect their cars. They could see from where they stood there was no way anybody could do that until the search was completed. The police, however, were wonderful to us. As soon as I mentioned that John's pills were in the car they organised for a police officer to go on to the course and get the pills from the boot and bring them back to me.

'We finally got the go-ahead to collect our car at about 4.45 p.m. After having left at 5.30 a.m. the previous day we finally got back home at 8 p.m. on the Sunday evening; and the story does have a happy ending because John did get to see the race. We all had to go to work on Monday, but Louise's father took him back up to Aintree; he was determined not to be beaten.'

Relieved and safe. A couple are re-united close to the first fence
(Stephen Shakeshaft, Liverpool Daily Post and Echo)

The Salvation Army provided welcome relief at Albert Dock
(Liverpool Daily Post and Echo)

Beans please! Stranded families tuck into breakfast at Fazakerley High School
(Liverpool Daily Post and Echo)

Mark and Beverley Power from Gloucester could only find a bed in the sauna at Feathers Hotel *(Liverpool Daily Post and Echo)*

Bedded down for the night. Racegoers in Everton Park Sports Centre
(Liverpool Daily Post and Echo)

Taking a nap after Sunday breakfast at Fazakerley High School
(Stephen Shakeshaft, Liverpool Daily Post and Echo)

Becher's Brook gets the once over from police search teams *(Bob Williams)*

Almost 6000 cars had to be meticulously searched
(Stephen Shakeshaft, Liverpool Daily Post and Echo)

Waiting to gain access to the racecourse on Sunday afternoon for their gear are *(left to right)* Brendan Powell, Richard Dunwoody, Charlie Swan, Jimmy McCarthy, Simon McNeill, Pip Hide, Jason Titley, David Casey *(behind Titley)*, Ken Whelan *(with helmet)*, Carl Llewellyn, Norman Williamson, Finbarr Leahy and Tristam Barry *(Pat Healy)*

At last! Racegoer Eric Gibbs is ecstatic about getting his car back on Sunday
(Liverpool Daily Post and Echo)

Armed police were present to protect the public
(Stephen Shakeshaft, Liverpool Daily Post and Echo)

Not even security guards avoided Monday's personal searching on arrival at the course
(Liverpool Daily Post and Echo)

Aintree's Managing Director Charles Barnett alongside Aintree's weighing room and the
plaque erected in honour of the people of Merseyside

* * * * *

Leading south coast flat race trainer John Dunlop and his wife Sue had decided that there could be no better way of celebrating son Harry's 21st birthday than to hold a party for him at Aintree on the 150th running of the National.

'All he thinks about is horses,' said Sue. 'We hired a glass-fronted box overlooking the start and invited 50 guests to what turned out to be a memorable day – but not quite in the way we had expected. We walked the course before racing and had enjoyed our lunch before the evacuation. Our guests were Harry's godparents, those who had helped him most with his racing, and many of his personal friends. Willie Carson and his wife Elaine were there as was Henry Cecil.

'We were herded out onto the track and then to the Melling Road. Like a lot of others I was desperate to go to the loo and I think I was one of the first to knock on a door and request the loan of their lavatory. I still had my empty glass in my hand and I left it with my hosts. Willie was soon to follow and I think he was quite glad to escape from the crush of autograph hunters.

'All our guests got home or to friends or hotels that night although some were very late indeed, after some terrible journeys. John and I were very lucky as by pure chance we fell upon our driver and car outside the course. We were driven to Manchester as planned and caught the last plane back to London, which was not long after six. Our guests managed to recover all their personal belongings, which was marvellous and we've had some ecstatic letters from Harry's friends. They, like us, had a day that they will never forget and perhaps strangely we all rather enjoyed it. The most amazing thing was, that as far as I could tell, no one felt nervous at any time.'

* * * * *

Jane Gerard-Pearse was looking forward to the Grand National more than most; it would be a fabulous day out with her husband Mike, five-month-old daughter Emily, and a group of family and friends. They were travelling to Aintree by helicopter from their home in the Derbyshire village of Parwich.

Jane's father also happens to be Stan Clarke, owner of Lord Gyllene, the eventual magnificent winner of the race, but not for another two days. Jane says: 'We travelled up in three helicopters, which took about 50 minutes, and there was great excitement to have a runner in the Grand National – it really was a dream come true, although I went along just hoping the horse would come back safe and we could have a nice day.

'We knew he could make the distance, and we knew he was well weighted but I think the Grand National is a bit of a lottery; all it takes is a loose horse or someone running across at Becher's for you to be out of it so, I don't think in our wildest dream we really thought it would happen, but we knew we were there with a fighting chance.'

The short journey for the party was followed by lunch in their private box in the Queen Mother's Stand, very close to the winning post. The excitement was building as the big event drew nearer.

'Mike and I went down to the saddling boxes and left Emily, who was asleep in her chair, with a friend,' said Jane. 'We were just watching Lord Gyllene being saddled up when the alarms went off. I said to Mike: "Quick, quick, go and get Emily". But by the time he had run back to the stand they wouldn't allow anyone in and the others had been cleared to the inside of the circuit while we went to the outside.

'They actually managed to get back to the helicopter and because of a bit of sneaky behaviour by the pilot they took off and left, they were very lucky to get away.

'The rest of us, of course didn't know anything about this and we had lost Mike. We hung around for about an hour, thinking it was going to be on, and finally we decided to walk around and try and signal to the helicopters so they could perhaps come out and meet us in a field or something.

'We tried every way we could think of to get into the course, as did a thousand other people. Dad even thought John Prescott might wield some influence, so he introduced himself and asked him to help, but of course he couldn't. We also tried to persuade a police sergeant who got very cross when Dad, very politely, asked him if there was a more senior person he could talk to.

'After a long walk we managed to see the in-field from the roadside, and we were horrified to discover all the helicopters had gone. Seven of us with no transport, the mobile phone not working and the prospect of a long night in Aintree.

'We eventually went to a house in Aintree Lane and my brother and I knocked on the door to ask to use their telephone. There was a couple with a young baby and quite sensibly they only allowed me in by myself. I phoned my parents' house to discover four of them had got home, including Emily much to my relief.

'We then got a number for the pilot, rang him and found out they were at Liverpool airport, which was about 25 miles away. They had to leave by 7 p.m., which left us about 40 minutes to get there.

'I went outside to tell the others and we were trying to work out how to get there with no taxis available. We noticed there were two cars on the driveway so we knocked on the door of the house again and she said: "I know what you're going to ask".

'They were absolutely lovely and took us in two cars, very fast round the back lanes and then on to the motorway and we made it with two minutes to spare, so we flew home. The shock afterwards was worse than during the day. I didn't sleep that night thinking about what could have happened to Emily with the fact a bomb might have gone off.

'Mike arrived back about two hours after us. He only had £8 in his pocket and was walking around trying to work out how to get home when a car pulled up and the driver said: "Look mate, you're going to get mugged. Don't walk around in this part of the city with a suit on."

'He took Mike to a taxi place and he managed to persuade them to take him back, promising to pay at the other end.

'That night we sat around discussing whether Lord Gyllene should run on the Monday – was he okay? Had the magic of the occasion been lost? Should we stand up and defy the miserable terrorists and return? We were all very deflated because this special day had turned into a nightmare. There was some hesitancy but then the doubts went because we might not get an opportunity like that again.

'We decided right; we're going to do it all again and we are going to enjoy it. In fact most of us wore the same outfits on the Monday, my sister Sally wore his colours of green and black. Some people couldn't go so eight us went back in two helicopters and we were lucky to land because of security surrounding the Prime Minister.

'We had the same box and when I went to the parade ring I took Emily with me. The atmosphere was fantastic, the magic was still there and the race itself was incredibly exciting.

'We have all seen enough Nationals where the horse has been beaten from the elbow, or the horse that looks as if it is running the best ends up tripping over. It's not over until it's over and even coming down the last few fences and the straight the volume in our box was unbelievable. He was running so freely, his ears pricked; he looked as if he could run it again.

'We whizzed down the steps with Dad – and I did leave Emily with someone in the box in all the excitement. It was a fantastic end and as we went to leave we realised Dad had forgotten the trophy so someone had to run back and collect that.

'When we came to land at home my other sister who couldn't come had got a great big sheet and drawn a horse with YES in great big letters next to it. In the corner it said Red Rum Mark II.'

7

The Mersey Beat

A S I have mentioned on several occasions, I have been involved with the National, Aintree and Merseyside for more than 20 years and as such have got to know the area pretty well and made some close friends. Strangely enough I had visited Liverpool on many business occasions long before I was involved with the National. Before joining Ladbrokes in the early '70s I was employed as advertising manager of Bath-based crane makers Stothert and Pitt. I knew nothing whatsoever about engineering but fortunately a little about marketing. One of this company's major customers was based at Liverpool Docks and we supplied them dockside and container cranes. This is probably as boring to you as it was for me, although there was the enormous benefit of living in the beautiful city of Bath. However, I was required to visit Liverpool quite often so there was no shock to my system when these visits became even more frequent after 1976.

The best way to get to Liverpool from the south is probably by train and then, if going to Aintree, you have the experience of a 20-minute taxi ride with an always entertaining Scouser cabby. Inevitably the conversation gets around to football and it's well to tread carefully until you have discovered if your driver is an Everton or Liverpool supporter. I can remember Ian Hargreaves of the *Liverpool Post and Echo* saying to me many years ago when I was urging him for more Aintree coverage, that unless it's wearing a blue or red shirt, you don't stand too much chance.

One of my best pals in Liverpool was Bob Azurdia, who was

a leading light on Radio Merseyside. Bob sadly died not long ago but I will never forget the help he gave us. Bob understood the value of the National to Merseyside and never flinched from his support of the race. Bob was a one-off and whatever the occasion always turned up in similar casual clothes. You can be sure that we always made him very welcome.

Nowadays we get tremendous support from our local media and both the *Liverpool Post and Echo* and Radio Merseyside played pivotal roles over our April weekend. It is thanks to the *Echo* that we have been able to illustrate so much in this book. It soon became clear that it would be a matter of which photographs to leave out.

I have had so many good times in Liverpool that it came as no surprise to me that the locals responded so wonderfully on 5 April. The stories I have heard are extraordinary and go on for ever, and in just about every case there is a tale that will live on with those involved. Goodness knows how many gallons of tea were consumed and loos visited and I dread to think what some household telephone bills were the following quarter. Politicians, sporting heroes, trainers, jockeys, racing officials, catering staff or racegoers, it really made no difference to the local residents, it was open house to everyone. Many people have told me that they will return to the National in 1998, not so much to see the great race, but more to visit the folk who had shown them so much kindness. Many of them plan to stay with their new-found friends.

It was fitting that Aintree chose to honour one such resident at their May fixture when the Carol Towner Spirit of Merseyside Novices Hurdle was run. Carol, a mother of six, turned her home just as many others had done, into a free bed and breakfast for beleaguered racegoers, an action which also won her a medal in a local newspaper competition.

Also, last September, Aintree hosted an open evening, thereby giving Charles Barnett and his team a chance to talk to and thank many of the local residents personally. To commemorate the occasion a plaque has been mounted on the wall of Aintree's famous weighing room as tribute to the people of Merseyside.

* * * * *

Colin Griffiths, his wife Pauline and mother-in-law Margaret Summerfield live barely a stone's throw from Aintree racecourse. Wander down the Melling Road and their smart terraced house faces you from across the street in Warbreck Moor. They have lived there for many years and, apart from their proximity to the great event, they have an added interest every April for the duration of the Grand National meeting. It started in 1972 when Pauline and Margaret were having a drink in a pub close to their home when a stranger approached asking for advice.

'Can you recommend anywhere to stay around here?,' asked the smartly-dressed young man.

'Why not come and stop at ours?' replied Pauline, not guessing who the figure was.

Twenty-five years later John Buckingham still knocks on the door at Warbreck Moor and is welcomed by the householders to stay for the week. That first visit was only five years after he had been riding 100-1 outsider Foinavon in the 1967 Grand National when, well off the pace, something alerted his attention in front. Running loose on the inside of the course going into the 23rd fence, Popham Down changed direction, running right across the front of the obstacle. In the resulting mayhem, which brought down every horse or prompted them to refuse, John Buckingham picked his way through the loose animals and jockeys to jump the fence and complete one of the most remarkable victories of all. Now he is a valet for the jockeys, his association with the race just as strong.

John was putting the final touches to the jockeys' riding gear while Colin and Pauline were in Tattersalls, just two of the thousands waiting for the race to start this unbelievable April day. 'We heard a sort of siren and thought it was a car alarm,' said Colin, a bus driver by trade. 'We couldn't see anything wrong and no one seemed to be too bothered until we heard *Operation Aintree, All Areas* over the tannoy.

'I looked round and saw the Queen Mother Stand emptying. The next thing there were police and mounted police telling us to make our way into the country. There was no mass panic, and as we got into the middle of the course a policeman told me there had been a bomb scare. The policeman was not entirely sure what was happening so was clearing everyone out.

'We thought we'd better get home quick because if Pauline's mother was watching the BBC she would be in a mad panic. When we got home we looked at the coverage and then went outside and sat on the wall watching the comings and goings. There seemed to be thousands of people.'

The family's proximity to the course gave them a grandstand view of the confused racegoers pouring out of the course; their racing connections were to lead to something else. 'I was stood at the gate and this fella walked up from the direction of the station and said: "Have you got any rooms?" I said: "Sorry mate, we're absolutely bulging." A couple were walking down the road and heard him and said: "Come to ours". And that was it, off they went. It was happening all over the place.

'John Buckingham came over with Gee Armytage, Andy Townsend – the lad who works with him who also stays with us – and another guy. Pauline asked them in for a cup of tea. By this time you couldn't see across the road there were so many people. There were jockeys and trainers and owners and all sorts. They all spotted John and came over the road and inside our house. Before we knew where we were there was a queue from the top of the stairs to the gate for the toilet. It was unreal.

'Gee said she was cold and came into the living room. Next thing she had her coat off, her shoes off and she was curled up on the couch. After that it was one continual stream of people coming and going; there was Simon Earle, Michael Caulfield, Richard Dunwoody, Andrew Thornton, Chris Maude and his wife and many others.'

The Griffiths' home was clearly attracting attention. Before long a group of newspaper reporters also walked through the open front door and begged to use the phone, desperate to impart what little information they knew back to their offices.

Colin, Pauline and Margaret were trying to keep pace with their visitors' needs, but they were helped out. 'Andrew Thornton went over the road and came back with about 20 portions of fish and chips and pie and chips,' recalls Colin. 'They were all tucking into those and Pauline put some biscuits out on a tray. Someone said they should replace all this and before we knew it the tray went round and we ended up with £80, which they gave us towards the phone calls and the hospitality. We didn't know what to say.

'At one stage every room was full; there was a jockey in the back bedroom having physio for a bad back. There must have been 40 to 50 people here; down the stairs, in the bedrooms, in the kitchen, on benches along the hall, on the wall outside, standing on the path. A bus came to a standstill at the top of Melling Road and people were taking pictures of our house because there were that many people standing around. It was chaos.'

Fortunately for the residents of the Warbreck Moor house, things eventually began to calm as their unexpected guests decided they would have to move on. 'The majority left between 6 p.m and 7 p.m. after ringing around to meet people,' said Colin. 'The police had blocked the roads off so they couldn't get through and they were on the phone arranging different places to go.'

Despite the departures, a group did stay the night. 'There was John and Andy, of course,' says Colin, 'and also another six. All four bedrooms were full, plus a mattress and a sofa bed in the living room. Another was flat out on the couch.

'No one could believe what had happened. People were saying: "We can't let them do it. Let's just go and run it anyway". Then they realised there may have been a bomb because of the controlled explosions. Then it was just a case of making the best of it.'

Sunday morning arrived and Colin wandered over the road to buy provisions to feed his assorted guests – and found some unexpected fame. 'We went over to the shop to get stuff for breakfast and as we were coming out one of the cable television stations was setting up and I did an interview with them.

'When we got home all sorts of reporters started arriving so we ended up cooking breakfast for them as well. All day Sunday there was a constant stream in and out because people were using us as a base by then.'

There was slightly more peace late on Sunday afternoon, but even then Pauline was kept busy. 'They had decided the race was definitely going to be run but all their cars and clothes had been stuck on the racecourse. We were literally taking clothes off their backs, washing them, drying them and putting them back on again. We even had ten people for the Sunday evening meal, so again we had to go out for extra food. Thank God, on Monday evening they all went home. It was enjoyable but exhausting.'

Colin, Pauline and Margaret were delighted when they were invited to Aintree for a celebration to thank the hundreds of people who had opened their doors to the needy and stranded. During the evening, Aintree's managing director Charles Barnett unveiled a tribute to his guests, a plaque which read: *This was commissioned by Aintree Racecourse Company Ltd as a mark of gratitude to all local residents who showed such hospitality to racegoers in need of help in the aftermath of the events of Saturday, 5th April 1997.*

'We didn't expect anything like that,' said Colin. 'When something goes wrong we just all pull together. Maybe now people will see Liverpool for what it is and not just what they used to think. People watch the news and read the paper and make their own minds up but to see what it is really like is something different.'

* * * * *

Every local authority is prepared for a disaster. They are, of course, never expected but that does not stop the teams in charge being on 24-hour alert. Chemical escapes, explosions, gas leaks and plane crashes are just a few of the problems they would know how to start dealing with in minutes of their occurrence.

Chris Turner is the grandly titled Deputy Chief Emergency Planning Officer of the Merseyside Fire and Civil Defence Authority's Emergency Planning Unit. It is a vital job, even if an almost continuous working life of being on standby and planning for the unexpected is his major role.

In Chris's past there has been a major fire at a chemical site in Cheshire when he thought he would have to oversee the evacuation of 10,000 people, but the trouble was averted. In February 1990, a day when Everton were playing football at

Goodison, an unexploded World War II bomb was discovered in Walton during drainage work; a few sports centres were opened in anticipation but again there was no full scale alert.

Despite these trial runs and others, Chris was confident his team would be able to cope with any eventuality. He has five officers, each looking after a region of Liverpool, and one is always on standby. On 5 April Fred O'Grady, the man from Knowlsey, was on duty, armed merely with his mobile phone.

'I was sitting at home watching the race on television,' said Fred. 'When they started evacuating from the stands I thought there was a chance I might get work. As soon as the second phase kicked in and they started moving people off the course, I got a phone call from police headquarters.'

That contact from Gold Command at Canning Place was initially to find out numbers for bus companies so the police could prepare themselves to shift thousands of people away from Sefton. Fred realised the operation was going to assume a much larger scale and so headed for the HQ himself. 'The police were in charge of this major incident and they wanted the emergency unit planning officer to provide information to secure additional support,' said Chris. 'The police, fire and ambulance were then able to do their normal jobs and we could go along and tell them how Liverpool could open up rest centres and accommodation and shelter and this sort of thing. We contact the other agencies to get their support.'

It was not just the buses Fred was trying to activate; it was clear many people would be wandering around the city with nowhere to stay for the night. Rest centres, in the form of sports halls and schools, would have to be opened and then blankets, food and refreshment would have to be provided. 'Once people are displaced it's the local authority's responsibility to offer temporary accommodation,' said Fred. 'All our contingency arrangements within each of the districts are capable of mobilising those locations and getting the staff out to open them and also to contact the voluntary organisations like the Red Cross to supplement our staff.'

When Fred arrived at Gold Command, all he knew were the basics of what was happening at Aintree. 'I didn't know whether the evacuation was temporary and the people would be moved back in again,' he said. 'But while I was travelling it was decided that a search would have to be made of the whole course, including the car parks. It was obvious that would take some time.

'By then some of the buses had arrived on site and the police were moving people down to the Albert Docks, which did subsequently cause problems. I got a briefing from the police and they said no one would be allowed back on the course that day. Armed with that information, I wanted to know the numbers involved.

'I decided that Liverpool and Sefton would have to open up the resources they had got – all of them.' Fred called his colleagues in each authority area and waited for the response. As soon as he had the information, he attempted to stop the evacuation to Albert Docks and to re-direct the stranded racegoers to the rest centres now under his command.

'It's amazing how it worked,' he said. 'There are so many multiple decisions and it was incredible how well it all came out because all the contingency planning had stopped once the people were evacuated from the grandstand; it was "busked" from that point onwards. We had locations being opened by Sefton and Liverpool and as they came on stream they were reporting back to us at our control point. I had a police superintendent and three or four PCs and in the end we commandeered an office which is usually used for the planning of football matches.'

Fred and his team were up and running. As more temporary accommodation around the city opened for the racegoing refugees, buses were instructed to head in their direction. What the emergency team had not bargained for was the generosity of the people of Liverpool; despite opening a host of sports centres and schools, only a small fraction of the available places were eventually needed.

Everton Sports Centre was the biggest holding area under Liverpool City Council's control that night, with 400 people staying. The Peter Lloyd Sports Centre catered for 115, Croxteth Sports Centre 50, Garston Sports Centre 64, Picton Sports Centre 57, Walton Sports Centre 150 and Park Road Sports Centre 100.

There were also many other buildings opened and either not used or any arrivals transferred. It was the same story in Sefton and Knowlsey and, amazingly, only 1,100 people were looked after by the local authorities that night, another testimony to the generosity of the people of Merseyside and the cramped conditions in certain hotels.

'We know how many people went into rest centres; they were an unknown number who went into homes,' said Fred. 'We had spare capacity. By 10 p.m. we were looking around for people. No one was presenting themselves. Our only problem was where were the missing people? Where had they gone? We were only handling a small fraction of them.'

Down at the Albert Docks many people were fed up with milling around and had headed off into the city to find pubs. Word soon spread that voluntary services were providing the stranded with free food at the Docks, and so Fred and his team maintained their search until well after midnight. By this stage, the ambulance service was also involved, picking up drugs from chemists and touring the centres to help people whose vital medical needs were locked in their cars.

Fred also paid tribute to BBC Radio Merseyside, saying: 'Without them there is no way we could have kept everyone informed. It was never an official option, it was just spontaneous.

'There was one strange irony in Knowlsey, where the Kirkby Civic Centre had 17 people staying. A coach had come down from Glasgow and half the people got off for a religious exhibition there, and the other half went to the Grand National. The coach was impounded so we had 17 people who had not even been to the races who had to be put up for the night.

'The atmosphere at headquarters was very good because we felt we were doing a good job. The co-operation from everybody was unbelievable. Nobody ever said no, no matter what. The local authorities got food from Tesco, Sainsburys and so on; no problem at all. Everything was available to us.'

* * * * *

Fazakerley Hospital drafted in extra staff once news of the

evacuation reached them as casualties suffering from shock and chest pains were ferried by ambulance to the accident and emergency unit. A bus crash close to the racecourse added to the chaos with a further 19 passengers needing hospital treatment.

Chris Pearce, director of nursing, said the hospital was in a semi-emergency state. 'We had about a dozen people from Aintree. Some people had medical conditions and were unable to get to their cars parked at Aintree, to get to their medication. Others, anxious about relatives, were suffering from chest pains.'

Ambulance crews were kept at full stretch as they dealt with the alert and the bus crash. A total of 15 paramedic units were on full standby at Aintree and chief executive David Todhunter said the whole operation came together like pieces in a jigsaw.

'The public should be commended on the way they evacuated. They responded extremely well despite not being able to use their vehicles. People had to walk a fair distance and some of them had heart conditions. There were others suffering dehydration because they had gone a while without a drink and some suffering from the effects of the cold.'

*   *   *   *   *

Peter Gill was the chairman of Aintree Parish Council in 1997 and his area, covering around 7,000 electors, included the famous racecourse. Despite being given tickets to go along on the Saturday afternoon, Peter, in engineering by profession, passed them on to his son and daughter-in-law and decided to follow the race on television. 'We watched the events and didn't know really what to do,' he said. 'There were an awful lot of people on the streets.'

Joan Harkins has been on the council for 14 years and she was driving home when she encountered the troubles; the police had closed the road and would not let her complete the few hundred yards left to her front door.

'But I only live in Aintree, why can't I go home?' Joan protested.

'What if the bomb's outside your house?' was the alarming response from the officer at the scene.

'I had no way of letting the family know where I was and finally got home about 6 p.m.,' said Joan. 'I had eventually got into the estate and parked on the outskirts and walked through. Well you can imagine there were hundreds and thousands of people, it was solid. It was quite frightening really because it was quiet, people didn't know what to do, it was awful. I thought to myself "I'd better invite these people in for a cup of coffee, they're freezing." Some of the girls were just in summer dresses. I got through the door and my husband said: "Are you all right, are you all right"' I just wanted to cry.'

Despite her emotional state, the thought of the beleaguered thousands outside soon focused Joan's attention. 'My son said a lady had been on the phone wanting to know if I could open the Methodist Church,' she said. 'I only run the Guides unit there but being on the parish council people turn to you for advice no matter what goes on.' Joan was immediately on the phone to Peter and to the church minister. He then contacted the committee before giving his approval to open one of the city's many refugee centres.

'I asked my husband to phone all our friends, asking them to bring a friend and asking them in turn to bring another friend,' said Joan. 'I didn't know how we would cope otherwise. My daughter and I ran down to a policeman on the corner of Aintree Lane and I told him we were going to open the church. I said we didn't want everybody there but if he saw elderly people or children just quietly tell them where they could find somewhere to go.

'We then went down to the church and put the urn on. We have a little cupboard where we keep drinks so I got half a dozen cups out.'

Joan was to be wildly out in her prediction of the numbers turning up at the Methodist church with its hall. While the hot water was heating up for supplies of tea, Peter was on his own mission to alert anyone he could find to the comfort being offered. 'I went down to the Ormskirk Road and told everyone the church was open and available for refreshments and it was warm and there was seating,' he said.

'From there I went to Asda in Aintree and asked if they could supply us with tea bags, coffee, milk sugar and so on and they kindly did. I also went to the food store just along the road and he was brilliant. He actually gave us eggs, bread, butter, cornflakes and so on and no charge at all.

'I went back to the church, came home to get my wife and then we decided to put it over the radio that the hall was available for anyone who wanted to come. There isn't a phone in the Methodist church so I had to give my home number out and more or less as soon as they gave it out over Radio Merseyside, the phone never stopped ringing.

'The first one was a lady from Crosby who used to live in Aintree and she was offering help. She apologised because of her name – which was Irish. She came along, an elderly lady, and she helped out in the evening and took four people back with her to put them up overnight.'

Joan, of course, was expecting a more leisurely influx. However, seconds after turning the tea urn to heat up, she recalls: 'All of a sudden we were inundated with people. I told them to sit by the radiators, and said we'd make them a cup of coffee. They were just dazed and I was in tears. They were asking how they were going to get home. They were in shock, it was horrible.

'Fortunately things got much better because all these people we had rung from home arrived and they brought coffee and sandwiches and cakes. It just snowballed from my half a dozen cups. Everyone just mucked in, they just got on with it, it was really lovely. We were also acting as counsellors – because they were with us most of the night they poured their hearts out; one man was telling us about his son being on drugs.'

Peter, meanwhile, was charging between the church, his home five minutes away in Uppingham Avenue, where his wife Beryl was taking the calls for help, and the search for lost souls. 'Someone phoned with the use of a caravan,' he recalls. 'They said it had got electricity and he took in two people and a dog and gave them the caravan and food.

'Early evening two couples arrived and the men went off to try and hire a car while the wives decided to stay. We didn't see them again until one in the morning and the women were frantic because they didn't know what the hell had happened. When they got back one of the wives burst into tears. It turned out they had tried to phone for a hire car, couldn't get one, so they made their way down to Liverpool airport, and they didn't have any cars there. They were told the nearest place to get one was Manchester airport, so they phoned and discovered there was one car left. They went to Manchester by train, picked the car up and drove back and met their wives, who thought they had probably gone off home on their own by then.'

The Methodist church continued to provide a safe haven until the early hours. Joan's half a dozen cups proved to be a little optimistic: 'We must have had 500 people or more during the evening,' she said. 'A brass band arrived, the Fishburn Band from Hartlepool. There were about 30 of them on a coach and were waiting for another one to pick them up. They were marvellous and said they would come back and play for us at any time.

'We also had two policemen at the church for a while and at one stage they said they wanted to shift everyone out to Liverpool because there was accommodation there. I told them there was no way these people were going anywhere until we knew exactly what was going on. We had discovered that some of the racegoers who were standing by the train station were moved out to Liverpool and then brought right back to us.'

Peter, the man who had given away his tickets and expected to watch the Grand National at home on television, was in for an unexpectedly long night – the last people out of the hall left at 4 a.m., having been promised a replacement coach which never did turn up. The locals, instead, set up their own taxi service to take the stranded party to a rest centre near by.

'We came back and opened the church at 8 a.m.,' he said. 'I toured the area again and told people the hall was open. Many of them came back for breakfast, including the couple who had gone and stayed in the caravan with the dog.'

* * * * *

Teresa Chadwick told her son Steven to have a good day at the races and wished him well with his betting, no doubt adding not to lose too much. As he walked the short distance from Ormskirk Road to the course, Teresa stayed at home preparing the evening celebrations, knowing her daughter was also due to arrive that night with a group of friends. As she was running around the kitchen, the phone rang, and Steven's urgent voice said: 'Mum, there has been a bomb scare.'

It took Steven and his party of friends and family an hour to get through the swollen streets back to his mother's house, where Teresa was viewing the mayhem. 'I was talking to people and the police helicopter hovered overhead telling everyone to leave,' she said. 'They found out they would not be allowed back on the course.

'At first it was like a party atmosphere, people sitting down outside having a picnic, asking how Everton were getting on! This went on for a while but after a couple of hours the atmosphere began to change and people got anxious.'

Steven soon understood the misery of the stranded, and decided to do whatever he could to help. 'I rang several mates and organised lifts to Haydock and local places like the station, the buses and so on,' he said. 'Anywhere local and we would take them. I told lots of people walking past that if they walked around the back I would arrange my friends to give them lifts – there must have been 100 people we sorted out.'

The generosity and the warm welcome from inside the house in Ormskirk Road was clearly tempting a group standing outside; but they appeared lost and confused. Despite the invitations, there was no response.

Steven said: 'After a while we discovered they were Czechoslovakians. They are very timid people and very shy. They were very reluctant to come in at first and have a cup of tea. They said nothing and just looked bemused.'

Teresa added: 'I phoned their hotel, the Springfield, and they asked me to look after our new guests until they called me back. They eventually came in and took their shoes off, even though we told them not to bother to do that. There were ten of them in each room and some in the conservatory.'

This new alliance enjoyed their evening together, despite the language barrier, and eventually Steven and his band of friends arranged to get them back to the Springfield Hotel. Teresa said: 'We felt so sorry for them, they were so far from home. We have received some lovely letters since and swapped photographs. I hope we will see them again next year.'

* * * * *

Costas Constantinou is the owner of the Olympic Fish and Chip bar in Aintree Way, just off the Ormskirk Road. It is a business which has been in his family for 24 years, providing take-away food, including Chinese meals, to the local residents. Grand National weekend is always a boom time because of their location a few hundred yards from Aintree.

Costas knew it would be a busy three days; particularly the Saturday with many of the 60,000 racegoers heading in his direction soon after the last race. He had not expected what was to happen this day.

'I was travelling into work and I heard on the radio the meeting had been abandoned and I knew there would be a surge of people,' he said. 'I got to Copy Lane police station and they had closed the road so no traffic could come into the area where my shop is.

'I had to abandon my car and run to work and when I got near the shop I couldn't believe my eyes: there was a queue of people from the door to the bus stop about 50 yards away. I was just gobsmacked. The shop was full to the brim with this big queue outside. Fortunately we had quite a lot of food prepared for a normal National Saturday, but this was incredible.

'Everything was being sold without stopping. We carry a reasonable stock of potatoes and fish and pies but it was all so intense because no one could go anywhere. They all wanted something to eat and drink and after an hour we started to run out of things. We went though our evening's stock of fish in two hours, and then our pies and that was it. Then our potatoes were being run through.

'It was mayhem but everyone was very good-natured considering they were expecting to get home and knew they wouldn't. I tried to get out to get more pies but it was impossible. It took me until 9 p.m. to get away. People were asking for chips and curry and chips and gravy but we had run out of plastic forks so people were buying them and either sharing forks or burning their fingers.

'Eventually I managed to get out and I ran to my car and drove to Crosby and started buying up knives and forks and fish and pies. When I got back people were still queuing for an hour. They showed a great spirit; they were all laughing and joking and sharing. It was really great to see it happening.'

Costas was relieved to see things calm down just before 11 p.m., when he and his staff could at last catch their breath. 'It was absolutely mayhem,' he said. 'There must have been well over 1,000 people, maybe 2,000; it was a hell of a lot of portions of chips.'

8

Martell

WHEN Ivan Straker persuaded the massive Seagram empire
to take on the sponsorship of the Grand National in 1984,
I wonder whether he ever believed that the race would still be
supported by the House of Seagram into the 21st century. After
the victory of Sir Eric Parker's Seagram in 1991 there was
realistically no way Seagram (the Distillers) could follow this.

The astute West Country trainer David Barons often tells the
story of how, on several occasions, he offered the horse to Ivan
Straker to run for the sponsor. This is certainly so but what is also
certain is that Ivan never seriously considered buying the horse.
Ivan is nobody's fool and he reckoned that if the horse was to do
any good on the racecourse the publicity spin-offs would
inevitably follow. How right he was, for not only did Seagram's
victory result in enormous publicity for the sponsor, but a great
many people assumed that the horse was owned by them.

I am really fond of David Barons and you have to give him ten
out of ten for trying as when Martell took over the race mantle
in 1992, he produced another New Zealand-bred horse with
chasing potential, Martell Boy. He has performed quite well
although I am sure David would not mind me saying that he is
never likely to come close to winning a National. David
contacted me on several occasions to see if Martell Cognac would
be interested in buying the horse but sadly for him the answer
came back just the same.

The Seagram sponsorship years were good ones for Aintree as
with such a commitment from a sponsor, the future of the
National was secure. Investments could be made in terms of

facilities, and the race programme could be re-developed in a major way. These were also the John Parrett years and John's vision was to build a racecourse and a race programme to rival Aintree's sister course, Cheltenham. Were he alive today John would be mighty pleased with the achievements and how others have continued on the great work he started.

There were some well-priced winners during Seagram's reign, including Last Suspect at 50/1 in 1985 and I know Ivan was particularly delighted that his friend and fellow officer in the 11th Hussars, Captain Tim Forster, had collected the spoils. Two years later nearly saw the greatest Grand National fairy tale of all time when The Tsarevich, owned by Ivan Straker, looked the probable winner as they approached the Elbow. The excitement in the Sefton Suite, where Seagram were entertaining their guests, must have been unbearable and after a titanic struggle up Aintree's heart-breaking run-in the brave Tsarevich was run out of it by the Toby Balding-trained Maori Venture, a 28/1 shot. Poor Ivan found it all too much to bear and to the absolute horror of everyone present, collapsed, suffering from a minor transient stroke. We were all delighted that Ivan made a complete recovery and is still an Aintree regular, and is one of the very few in racing to have been honoured with a life membership to the course.

It was typical of Ivan and Seagram's generosity that the following year they commissioned Philip Blacker to sculptor a magnificent life-size bronze of Aintree's greatest hero Red Rum, which was unveiled shortly before the 1988 Seagram Grand National by Her Royal Highness The Princess Royal. The next time she was to honour Aintree with her presence was in 1997.

After the Seagram victory the group decided that, while it wished to retain corporate involvement with the National, it would be preferable if the sponsorship was used to promote a specific brand. For those of us closely involved with the event it was always slightly puzzling that Seagram had decided to sponsor under their corporate identity. Not that we were complaining, of course, but it was rather incongruous that you could not buy a bottle under the Seagram name, certainly not in the UK.

The House of Martell, distillers of one of the world's leading brands of Cognac, were to take over as sponsors of the three-day meeting and to announce the event Martell invited the media to a unique press conference at their magnificent Chateau de Chanteloup in the heart of Cognac. This was quite some occasion and rather set the seal on the style of operation that is associated with everything Martell do. They really are quite magnificent sponsors and wonderful people to do business with. Wonderful does not mean easy, for the Martell executive are tough negotiators, but once terms of reference are agreed they do everything in their power and everything their budget allows to help promote the meeting worldwide. They make friends wherever they go within racing and, as a result of their gentle and discreet handling of the media they have established the Martell Grand National as the accepted title of the race.

Everything Martell do, they do with great style. The Charity Ball they sponsored and organised at London's Dorchester Hotel in April 1997 to commemorate the 150th running of the race was thought by many to be one of the finest and most stylish racing evenings ever staged.

Martell back their prize money contribution of close to half a million pounds with a similar investment in the worldwide promotion of the event. In the UK their advisors are Rob Mason and Corinne Young of SBI, a sports sponsorship agency, and we work very closely with them throughout the year. It makes everyone's life a great deal easier when individuals work well together with one common aim. This is how it is with Corinne and Rob with our single aim being a successful Martell Grand National Meeting.

One of the most important markets for Martell is the Far East and they use the Martell Grand National as a promotional vehicle throughout these territories. The main thrust of the activity is the live satellite transmission of the National to the Hong Kong Jockey Club either at Sha Tin or Happy Valley racecourses. An extraordinary amount of work precedes this transmission and Cantonese commentators travel over to Aintree to enhance the enjoyment of the occasion for the thousands of racegoers who stay on to watch the event in Hong Kong. As a reciprocal arrangement two Martell sponsored races are transmitted to the UK and are shown to the Aintree racegoers prior to the start of racing on Grand National day. SIS, who assist us in the co-ordination of both these transmissions, also broadcast these two Hong Kong races to their 10,000 or so betting shop subscribers in the UK, Ireland and Europe.

Every year, Gerry Morrison of the BBC's television sports team produces a promotional video in conjunction with Rob Mason of SBI, for Aintree and Martell and this always shows scenes from the Hong Kong racetrack. The excitement the race generates over there is truly amazing and it attracts an extraordinarily large betting turnover even though there is no jump racing in that part of the world. Naturally the occurrences of both 1993 and 1997 were nothing short of disastrous as far as betting was concerned. I believe these are the only two occasions in the history of the Royal Hong Kong Jockey Club where all totalisor stake money has had to be returned in full to the punters. Also Martell were naturally extremely concerned about any adverse effects this may have had on their business. The question had to be asked: 'Should we be associating ourselves with an event which has failed to take place on the day scheduled on two of the six occasions that we have sponsored it?'

On the plus side as far as Martell were concerned was the fact that the two Nationals in question have certainly received more publicity than any others in living memory. Couple this with the fact that Martell themselves were in no way to blame for any of the occurrences in either year, and overall the publicity they, as a company, received was very much of a positive nature. Such is their strength of resolve and their commitment to the Grand National and Aintree Racecourse, that their support has never outwardly wavered. Furthermore in September of 1997 they were delighted to confirm their intentions to continue their sponsorship until well into the 21st century. Aintree, and indeed racing as a whole is very lucky indeed to have the backing of such a professional and totally motivated organisation.

BBC Television Sport have played a major role in the continued strengthening of Martell's position. We believe that the partnership that has built up between organiser, sponsor, and broadcaster is unique within British sport. So much so that personal friendships have developed and throughout all our dealings an enormously strong bond has been built on these friendships, coupled with professional respect and mutual trust. Such is the nature of Martell and the attitude of their executives, that never for one minute would they even contemplate abusing this situation. Generally speaking they would not ask any favours, although a favour was asked of the BBC on one memorable and hopefully unique occasion in 1996.

In that year, owing to the construction of the fixture list, the Martell Grand National meeting fell in the month of March – nothing to worry about so far. We were finalising all our satellite bookings for the simulcast to Hong Kong, when we suddenly realised to our absolute horror that we would still be on GMT, when usually we would be on BST the clocks having gone forward one hour at the end of March. The consequence of this was that the race would be seen in Hong Kong one hour later, so late in fact that no right minded individual could be expected to hang around to watch it.

Judith Menier, Martell's international public relations director, is our main contact throughout the year. The Grand National sponsorship is very much her baby and she knew that if the Grand National was to be run at the time it was currently scheduled, Hong Kong would not transmit it and Martell's whole Eastern marketing rationale would be damaged. It was decided that Aintree and Martell would firstly approach Dave Gordon and Martin Hopkins of BBC Grandstand and then head of sport Brian Barwick to see if the race could be run at 3 p.m. rather than the usual slot of 3.45 p.m. We knew this would require major rescheduling and would upset a lot of the plans the BBC already had in place. Aintree agreed to assist in any way we could and, by starting the race programme ten minutes earlier, we could hold two races before the National and move the original first race to become the fourth at 3.45pm.

The point of this tale is to illustrate the strength of the relationship that I have just referred to, for, within 24 hours, the BBC had a new timetable and were able to agree to the request. The 1996 Martell Grand National would be run as the third race on the card at 3 p.m.

It was understood by all parties that the race time would revert to 3.45 in 1997 which suited Aintree, as an earlier start time is not ideal when trying to bring in 60,000 racegoers and it is deemed far more sensible to hold three races before the big one, thereby building up to your main attraction.

Martell and indeed Seagram corporate use the Grand National as a major hospitality vehicle inviting personalities, customers, guests and friends from all over the world. Similarly Martell host customer functions in many other countries where the race is transmitted. This extends from casinos in Russia to racing clubs in Bombay, with of course the major function taking place at either Sha Tin or Happy Valley in Hong Kong.

At Aintree guests were being entertained in grand style in several function rooms including the two tier Martell Pavilion, which is purpose built and reflects Judith and her team's exquisite taste. The Pavilion is superbly sited close to both the start and finish of the great race and houses an incredible 400-plus guests. Getting this huge number of people from all over the globe to and from the races is a huge logistical task. Martell employ specialists to handle the exercise and it involves transport by plane and helicopter, by sea, by train, both scheduled and charter, by special coaches and hire cars.

Imagine therefore the situation that Martell were faced with when their guests were evacuated to different parts of the racecourse and different streets outside the course. How could they locate them all, ensure that they were all safe and get them back to their hotels, stations or airports and home? I should think there is a book to be written covering this alone, as from what I understand there were some extraordinary experiences to say the least.

* * * * *

The delightful Judith Menier, natural smile permanently in place, was enjoying herself as much as anyone can when charged with the responsibility of looking after her company's most important guests from all over the globe.

Martell do not underplay the Grand National. It is their event; they plough millions into ensuring its continued success. Their clients and friends look forward to a fabulous outing each year; without Martell, the Grand National would be missing more than a sponsor's signature.

Judith, full of nervous energy, was in the Sefton Suite of the County Stand. Gathered around her were Patrick Martell, the president of Martell Cognac, and 70 of his most favoured family, friends and business contacts. There were top names from industry along with those more recognisable, including the actor Gregory Peck and his wife. Outside in the pavilion, another 420 of Martell's guests were gathered to enjoy the day. It was not the time for anything to go wrong.

'I was in the Sefton Suite because we were expecting the Princess Royal to come along fairly soon,' said Judith. 'Then our security consultant came over and said he had to have a word with me. "You should know there has been a coded call," he said, "but don't worry about it. We are going to wait and see what the Princess Royal's people do."

'I was obviously extremely concerned,' recalls Judith. 'I went off to find David McEwan, our vice-president of marketing and sales. It took me about ten minutes to get to him because he was on the other side of the Sefton Suite and I was stopped for a chat by nearly everyone in the room on the way over there.

'I didn't want people to see I was concerned. I took David aside to tell him what had happened and the alarms went off at the same time. There were 40 or 50 people in there at the time, all our VIP guests. When the alarms went off we just asked people, very calmly, to kindly leave. They all did so very quietly, some gathered their coats and we actually managed to empty the room very quickly.'

Even in the face of such a daunting task, Judith managed to find a humorous side to the mounting crisis. She said: 'There is an Irish priest, John Byrne, a family friend of mine who married my parents and buried them both as well. He comes to the Sefton Suite every year. Father John has never had an invitation but manages to walk through all the security and the police. He is very old now and not that good on his feet and he was sitting down at the end of the Sefton Suite watching television. David and I looked round and decided everybody had left and then all of a sudden we saw Father John calmly watching television and we had to go back, pick him up and put his coat on and take him downstairs.

'At that stage I presumed we would be evacuating for 30 minutes and everybody would be allowed back in. I went downstairs and most of our guests were standing just outside and the police were trying to move them away. David Hillyard came along and I was wondering what I should do next. David asked me to go to Charles Barnett's office and at least I thought I would be able to do something positive rather than just standing around.'

Ian Harris, the marketing director of Seagram UK, had an equally unenviable task. 'I was in the Martell Pavilion when it all happened,' he said. 'As soon as I heard, I had the microphone in my hand and made the announcement about everyone leaving.

'I was fully expecting us to evacuate out to the front, on to the racecourse and ten minutes later we'd be back in to watch the racing. That's why people didn't take coats, left things on the back of chairs which, in hindsight, of course was a mistake. None of us in our wildest dreams thought we wouldn't be able to get back in.

'It was a fairly casual reaction. The foreign visitors were confused. We had 420 guests in there but the problem was that we were evacuated to the front and some people who were downstairs went out of the back. When we got on to the racecourse the police were fanning us out and we got completely split up. Once that happened we couldn't get any messages out to co-ordinate anything because there were no phones or anything.'

Judith managed to scramble her way up to Charles Barnett's office. She was joined in there by the Aintree directors and senior management. David Hillyard announced very quickly he was going to phone Hong Kong because it was realised there was no way they would get the race on time.

'The discussion was still going on about how late we could run the race,' said Judith. 'We stayed in there until the police came back for a second time and said we had to leave.

'That was fine until we got outside and they started yelling "run, run". And the police were running as well. That was the only time I felt fear because I realised they really were expecting something to explode. We ran all the way to the back of the course and went to the police headquarters.

'By this stage I realised I didn't have my radio with me and the phones would not work. From then on it was one of the most frustrating things I have ever lived through because I couldn't actually do anything; I didn't know where anyone was. I was eventually able to call our office on the course and much of the team was still in there. The police obviously didn't realise. At 3.55 p.m. when we all ran out our security team just sat down in their Portakabin by the entrance to the County Stand. To be quite honest they could have been blown away.

'My assistant was also there. They stayed until about 11 p.m., which at least meant we had a control point and they were talking to the rest of the Martell team, finding out where everyone was. Patrick Martell was allowed to walk back to the office as well as he was very concerned about the situation and wanted to see for himself how things were going. One of the guys went up to a policeman and told him who Patrick was and he was allowed back on the course. It was amazing because when I asked to go there I was told absolutely no way.'

Ian had equally complicated problems, just on a much larger scale. 'I ended up in a small group because I was the last one to leave the pavilion,' he said. 'Everyone else had gone, a bit like the captain leaving a sinking ship. I wanted to make sure everyone was out before I left. Everyone had gone, including my wife who I didn't see again for 15 hours. I was left with one of our security guys who I tagged on to because he had a walkie-talkie, and two other guests.

'We moved on to the racecourse, bumping into other people, and the group got bigger and bigger. After an hour and a half we joined up with another big group as we walked up the Melling Road. We picked up more and more people and by the time we got to the end I guess there were about 190 of us.

'The problem was we had several different nationalities; some people spoke no English, some people spoke very little English. A lot of people weren't dressed to be outside on an April day in Liverpool, they were planning to be always under cover. It was getting cold and started to rain and no one knew what was going on.'

Inger Ward was one of the official Martell guides charged with looking after the VIP guests. As people were removed from the course, she decided to search for anyone wandering around. Incredibly, she stumbled across Gregory Peck and his wife sitting forlornly by the roadside with some other Seagram guests. Despite sporting a beard, wearing dark glasses and a hat, Gregory was still instantly recognisable in the midst of the crowds, and Inger knew she would have to act fast to look after the octogenarian actor.

She spied a second-hand car dealer across the road and just as she was about to approach and attempt to do a deal to borrow a car, a taxi came along, distinctive in the extreme by its psychedelic colouring. Inger waved down the driver and pleaded for some of her guests, naturally including the Pecks, to be taken to the airport where they could link up with the Martell planes.

'It'll cost yer,' exclaimed the driver in a broad Irish accent.

Inger bundled Gregory and his wife into the back of the cab and told the driver to 'get us out of here'. As he manoeuvred the grateful passengers at high speed through the cordoned off roads, he caught sight of the actor in his rearview mirror.

'Bejesus, if it's not Gregory Peck. I love your films,' he yelled. 'Can you put your signature on one of my taxi receipts?' Gregory, the epitome of charm and graciousness throughout the ordeal, went one better, taking the driver's address and promising to send him a signed photograph.

As the journey continued, Inger alerted airport security about who was arriving in the multi-coloured vehicle, and as they arrived the security gates opened and he was able to drive the film star on to the tarmac and right up to the steps of the private jet.

Judith was relieved by the fact her security team were able to discover where many of the guests were located. 'It was mind boggling,' she said. 'How were we going to get our guests to the station and on to our specially chartered train? The coaches were no good because we couldn't get them out. Fortunately, the VIPs on two private jets at Speke managed to filter back, bit by bit. There was nothing I could do so it was a matter of waiting for things to sort themselves out. I remember thinking this is what war must be like. You don't really know what is going on, where people are.'

Judith decided the best option was to head off to the Gold Command centre, and she was taken on a journey she will never forget. 'I don't like cars anyway and I just couldn't look,' she recalls. 'I remember seeing the back of a bus coming up very fast and after that I closed my eyes. I do remember thinking it would make great dinner party conversation.'

'I got down to the police station but that was rather frustrating because their phones didn't work very well either. People couldn't phone directly in and we couldn't dial directly out. But at least my mobile was working by then. People from all over the world were calling because they had seen what happened on the television.'

By then, Martell had already agreed to sponsor the race should it be run again on the Monday afternoon, and Judith attempted to contact her company executives to ensure they knew about it. 'Every Seagram executive I spoke to was extremely supportive,' she said. 'They all insisted: go for Monday, don't worry, these things happen. They really were superb and I was able to get in touch with almost everybody. By this stage our communications network was working well and we were slowly piecing together a clearer picture.

'Having been through the 1993 situation it wasn't very pleasant because we had already been through one crisis at Aintree. It was worse than 1993 because all my guests were outside, about 100 of them didn't speak English, didn't know their way about, it was very cold and damp. I felt terrible for all these people who were supposed to have a great day out and there was no way of getting them home quickly. I had a terrible feeling of responsibility but couldn't actually do much for people out in the streets.'

Ian was trying to take matters into his own hands. 'Communications were very, very sporadic,' he said. 'It needed someone to take control so I stood on someone's garden wall and I shouted: "This is a message to the Martell guests. I can't tell you anything but just to let you know we are trying to get more information. Please be patient and I will give you more news as soon as I have it".

'I got a rapturous round of applause because someone had actually said something, so I was given with the mantle of spokesman. The next time I got some information I persuaded a policeman to let me use his PA system so I made an announcement over his megaphone, saying: "We can't do anything but we must stick together."

'I went into the British Legion club opposite, where some of our people had drifted into. I saw they had a second bar and I asked if we could rent that room. Unfortunately they couldn't let us do it because of a function so we all headed into the main bar.

'Someone suggested the BBC catering tent, so after some discussion they allowed us to use it. So my guests actually came back on to the racecourse. Once we got people settled a security guy and I went off to find a way of communicating with the Gold Command. We were told to make our own way to Liverpool with the guests and I said: "I can't do that. I can't shepherd 190 people to the city."

'I had been told the queue was still over 10,000 people at the station and at this stage our charter train was still waiting for us at Lime Street. As far as I knew, there wasn't a problem. It was going to wait and as long as people knew they would get home eventually, spirits were fine.'

Unfortunately for Ian, that situation changed somewhat dramatically when staff at Lime Street decided the train could not be held up. With a smattering of Martell guests, and a whole lot more uninvited passengers who had managed to clamber aboard, the train left for London, giving the usual high-class food and drink to a train full of bemused and grateful racegoers.

Ian tried to find an alternative. 'Between 8 p.m. and 9.30 p.m. we had discussions with the coach company and the police agreed they would sweep the coaches but they wouldn't let them out in daylight. If they did that all the other coaches would want to leave. But we were assured there was a possibility of coaching people down to London.

'Someone pointed out that the drivers had already driven their hours. It was agreed they could drive the coaches out but they couldn't go further than Liverpool or somewhere close.

'We had ups and downs – yes we could get back to London, no we couldn't. Once we knew that we could get people on the coaches I made sure they got on them pretty quickly.'

The brightest spot of Ian's day then occurred. All his guests were on coaches but nowhere to go. He was trying to weigh up all the possibilities when his mobile phone rang; the then managing director of Seagram UK, Gordon Hessey, had managed to hire a Virgin South West train with his platinum American Express Card. 'It was real Dunkirk spirit,' said Ian. 'I made the announcement that we had got a train. A cheer went up as if England had scored the final goal in a World Cup final. It was after 9.30 p.m., everyone was tired. The police let us out and we trundled off to Lime Street station, about six coaches. Then we got information that the charter train had no food or drink on it and it had to leave by 10.30 p.m.'

Not blessed with the time or the facilities to conjure up the normal Martell hospitality, Ian thought on his feet. 'It was about 10.10 p.m.,' he said. 'There were a couple of kebab shops round the corner from the station. I always have a cash float with me and so I went in one and said: "Give me what you can, you've got ten minutes." The man gave me a funny look until I pulled a wad of £20 notes out and he realised I was serious, and they started cooking.

'I have never seen two guys galvanise themselves so quickly; they were cracking out kebabs, grills, frying chips. I sent the security guys back three times with trays of soft drinks. After 12 minutes I was checking my watch because obviously I didn't want to miss the train. Eventually five minutes before the train was due to leave I said: "Right, that's it. Stop cooking. Count all your bags, how much do I owe you?" I paid him for it, about £200 I suppose. They had been turning people away from the door as they were doing it.

'I ran back to the train and although there wasn't enough food to go round, most people shared something or other.'

Ian joined the train back to London with most of the sponsors' guests now accounted for; Judith stayed the night in St Helens, already worrying about how the next two days would unfold.

'It was a great boost to everyone's morale when the Princess

Royal said she would come back on the Monday,' said Judith. 'Bit by bit things began to get better. When I got to the hotel everybody was sitting in the separate hospitality area; my team and some guests. I had a glass of wine and about five minutes later the hotel got a bomb alert. I thought "This is not happening." Security said, "Don't move, we'll sort it out," and fortunately it was not a coded call but someone messing about. Mentally I was absolutely exhausted.

'I had nothing in the hotel. My bag was in one of the cars. I had my best suit on and that was it. I was very depressed about the whole incident, we didn't know who had managed to get home, who we had lost.

'Next morning I asked one of my colleagues in corporate communications for Seagram in London to go down to the Carlton Tower and do a headcount to see where people were. We had guests from the Czech Republic, from Poland, from South Africa and Singapore and I had no idea if they had all got back. We needed to be sure that they had all got back to London safely and I was very relieved to find out that everyone had got back that night. Then we had the huge question of how we got personal property to everybody. Eventually we did it on Monday, tagging everything after making paper labels with bits of string. It was a great experience when the race was run, the atmosphere was electric.'

Ian, however, had one more idea to make sure the people of Liverpool were rewarded for their hospitality and their help to 60,000 bemused racegoers.

'I was booked on a flight to go back to Manchester to watch the race and as I was packing my bag I thought: "Hang on". I told one of the managers who works with me on Martell: "I want to buy the people of Liverpool a drink. You can do it." I said "I'll leave it with you and I'll be back tomorrow."

'We selected the pubs and clubs we already had contact with through our sales force and we put an advertisement in the *Liverpool Echo* offering the people of Liverpool a free drink of Martell.

'Monday was superb, the racecard was already printed. It was amazing and I was just bowled over. It was a brilliant finish to the weekend.'

162

9

The BBC

THE Martell Grand National is a major jewel in the BBC's crown. As far back as I can remember our relationship has been unbelievably cordial and all of us at Aintree have built up friendships which are unlikely ever to be tested.

We work closely with the Beeb throughout the year and their help in promoting the National meeting and thereby supporting the magnificent contribution of sponsors Martell Cognac is immeasurable. It is of course the very strength of such a relationship which proves invaluable in an emergency or at a time of crisis.

After the events of 1993, the Aintree management have spent considerable time and energy in preparing specific contingency plans to cover the seemingly unlikely need to re-schedule the National. A Monday National has always been an option and indeed in 1994, when heavy rain throughout National week terrified the life out of us, a postponement to Monday was a distinct possibility. The BBC have to be heavily involved in all discussions of this kind as a Grand National without live television coverage would obviously be unacceptable.

Soon after key Aintree personnel had gathered together to discuss the consequence of the telephoned bomb threats with police chiefs, I was asked by Charles Barnett to get to the broadcast office as quickly as possible to ensure that the correct announcements were made and that the right messages appeared on all closed circuit screens throughout the track.

As I moved behind the Winners' Enclosure I caught the eye of Owen Thomas, the ubiquitous BBC floor manager. 'We need you on now,' he called. 'Give me one minute,' I replied. Rushing to the broadcast office, I gave Bob Cox and his team the required instructions, made sure everything was clear, and went back to join Desmond Lynam in the Winners' Enclosure. As I talked to Desmond we watched the early consequence of the announcements on his monitor. Although it was too early to say, I was as near certain as I could be that what I was watching meant the end of racing for the day. The only consolation (if you could call it that) was that the crowds were evacuating quickly and calmly and with an apparent lack of real anxiety. After 1993, what in God's name had we done to deserve this?

The BBC kept on broadcasting for as long as they were allowed from their position adjacent to the Winners' Enclosure but before long the whole entourage, Desmond et al, were moved on by the police and made their way to the jockeys, trainers and horsebox park. All their high-tech, very expensive equipment was left unmanned where it stood – it was a truly amazing sight. Owing to the foresight of BBC cameraman Howard Woosey, who rolled up a length of cable and carried it off with him, very soon the BBC were in the position of broadcasting from the car park where there shortly followed some dramatic interviews. Howard Woosey performs a unique function at Aintree. He is just about the only person other than jockeys, valets and officials allowed in the hallowed changing rooms during the build-up to the big race. With his hand-held camera, he has captured some moments of great emotion and high drama, yet he never abuses his privileged position.

So, thanks to Howard's forethought, Desmond talked live to leading jockeys and trainers, including a moving piece with Jenny Pitman, with Julian Wilson and lastly the extraordinary exchange with Charles Barnett where the real seriousness of the situation was emphasised for perhaps the very first time. The message from Charles was clear and concise: *everyone must leave, and leave now.*

The BBC transmission from Aintree was then suspended, but not before an extraordinary commentary from Jim McGrath, who was able to report from his perch at Becher's Brook working from his monitor. Since the meeting I have watched this many times; Jim talked for around 15 minutes describing the dramatic scenes as they unfolded. I reckon this was his finest hour, for although he will have many more opportunities to shine throughout his career, I doubt if there will be any quite so emotional and demanding. He managed to bring the sheer drama of the occasion right into the sitting rooms of the many millions watching around the world.

Later on and throughout the late afternoon and evening I knew I would have to keep in very close contact with the BBC regarding the re-scheduling of the race. Producer Martin Hopkins, with whom I have worked for 20 years, furnished me with various phone numbers and urged me to call him at any time. He and *Grandstand* editor Dave Gordon, along with most of the other key BBC management, would return to their hotel to await any news.

I can't exactly remember how many times I did actually call, but I know it was several. The BBC had really got their act together and were able to react swiftly to all our requests. The most crucial decision they were able to make was that Monday would be fine and they would come on air at 4 p.m., run until 5.30 p.m., with the live transmission of the Martell Grand National taking place at 5 p.m.

Having been forced to abandon most of their gear, particularly the heavy stuff, the safety of their equipment was obviously of major concern to the BBC engineering team and particularly their manager and technical co-ordinator Steve Whitaker. When you consider that they had some 40 cameras and 50 miles of cable, no end of mobile equipment and hundreds of meters of scaffolding, it is not difficult to understand the magnitude of the task before them.

On Saturday, after the evacuation, Steve was anxious to get round his equipment and in particular the cameras, as rain was forecast. At around 6.30 p.m. the police agreed that two, and only two, engineers could go out onto the course under escort but without transport. Steve also tried to retrieve Peter O'Sullevan's belongings from the top of the County Stand but there was no way this was going to be allowed on Saturday.

In actual fact, unbeknown to most, the BBC did actually

transmit from their scanner on Saturday evening straight into the main news programme. The camera overlooking the parade ring had been left on a wide angle and evocative pictures of the Ormskirk Road were transmitted. Also the camera in the weighing room had been left on remote and this enabled more dramatic shots to be broadcast. The deserted weighing room was a staggering contrast to the frenetic scenes of around 3 p.m.

On Saturday, Steve sent his London crews to Cheshire where they found hotels, whilst the Manchester-based contingent were taken back by bus. The McDonalds on the Ormskirk Road was used as the meeting point.

The main BBC controls, including the scanners, are sited in the horsebox park, so when this area had finally been declared sterile on Sunday, at least Steve and his large team were able to return to their HQ. There are a staggering 120-plus operatives under Steve's wing, but as he points out two per camera totals 80 before you think about the engineers, riggers and the rest.

Steve was getting very worried as time passed by on Sunday morning and still the crews could not get back on to the course to check through the equipment. Four or five hours had gone by since they reported for duty at 9 a.m. and by now Steve was seriously doubting whether the BBC would be able to transmit on Monday. A hastily convened meeting between the then Head of Sport Brian Barwick and Malcolm Kemp, the racing producer, with Chief Inspector Sue Wolfenden and Inspector Ken Laidler was able to reinforce how critical the situation had now become. Some time before 4 p.m. the permission that Steve was waiting for was granted, although he had to wait a good while longer before he could get men on to the County Stand.

On Monday Steve was less than amused that his staff canteen had been converted into a search control point. Finally he was able to repossess the canteen but not the tables which had been commandeered for security use. Steve's operatives had to eat their lunch with plates on laps but in the context of what had been going on since mid-afternoon on Saturday, it was not too much of a hardship.

Steve told me later on that the Beeb had actually lost one small camera and some microphones out on the course. However, I have since heard from him that these had been stored away and were safely recovered. Things had been pretty stressful for Steve and his team, but one thing's for sure: it could have been one hell of a lot worse.

* * * * *

Desmond Lynam, the most urbane of television hosts, puts the Grand National amongst his most favourite of tasks for the year. Under that charming and suave exterior, Desmond is still a journalist and nothing pleases him more than getting to grips with the great steeplechase and all the dramas and stories it almost inevitably produces. With the pomp and ceremony out of the way, there is then the blood and the guts of the horses and jockeys, the elation and sadness of the trainers, the tales of the owners.

Although Des does not present the Thursday and Friday BBC transmissions from Aintree, he is not resting. From his room at the Atlantic Towers Hotel in the middle of the city, he is reading, revising, researching and writing up notes on all the runners in the great race, trying to find different angles behind the runners and riders, where the horses were bought and by whom; were they a gift from someone which will turn out to become a lifetime memory? All this while keeping one eye on the television coverage, ensuring nothing develops which he has to be aware of.

'I used to go up to Liverpool early in the week,' says Desmond, whose first Grand National for television was in 1985, having covered many more for radio. 'But now I stay at home and go up on Thursday. I do a lot of homework for it so I'm familiar with jockeys, trainers and runners. I haven't got much chance to look at notes and things when I'm out in the open. There are a lot of people around me and they are deflecting my concentration so I've got to embed a lot the information in my mind.

'I don't go racing every week, I'm not a familiar with the subject matter as are the Richard Pitmans of this world, the people doing it day in, day out. I've made the mistake in the past of going to the race on the Thursday and Friday and you get caught from pillar to post by all the people and you don't actually concentrate on what you are trying to pick up.'

This does not mean Des is not involved in the planning; many months before the April event he and the *Grandstand* executives meet to discuss any possible stories which might crop up from the race, they consider how the build-up should go on the day, decide which horses, yards and jockeys to feature and to film for the previews.

While Des goes through his routine meticulously, the BBC team, under the guidance of *Grandstand* editor Dave Gordon, executive producer Martin Hopkins and racing producer Malcolm Kemp, are ensuring their side of the camera will run without hitch. Martin has been a *Grandstand* producer since 1977 and first worked on the Grand National as a floor manager in 1968. He was involved in the planning in 1990 when the race was deemed to have become so big, that it was no longer a mere outside broadcast with the rest of the show run from Television Centre in Shepherds Bush, but the whole programme moved up to Liverpool.

'That was the start of doing superb re-runs of the race and having cameras in a whole multitude of places that had not even been thought of,' he recalls. 'Now we go up to Aintree on the Tuesday for the rehearsal and we are on the air Thursday, Friday and Saturday. There are some who take the view that the first two days are a rehearsal for the Grand National, but we believe it has got to be excellent over the three days.'

The *Grandstand* transmission starts at 12.15 on the big day, but work starts long before, many of the team covering the breakfast at Aintree, where horses and some trainers parade, others checking through the technical side of the operation. 'I'm on site by 8.30 a.m. worrying about the day coming up, in company with everyone else,' says Martin. 'The videotape team have been working throughout the night preparing all the bits and pieces which go into the run-up to the race and the programme. Real rehearsals began at about 11 a.m., with Desmond Lynam, all the presenters and reporters, and checking that the video tapes and graphics are working because they are very complicated, all computer driven.

'That is done from my scanner and at the same time Malcolm Kemp is doing the equivalent in the race scanner, checking all the cameras and all the roving vehicles and making sure the links are working properly and all the sound circuits from the various sites within the course. It's a boring routine which has to be gone through and anyone who thinks they can do without it falls flat on their face on the day.'

With all the planning and the rehearsals done, the BBC's build-up to the Grand National 1997 went extremely well, delighting Martin and Dave. The preparation appeared to pay off and the hours before the race was due to start included pictures from the early morning gallops, a tribute to Peter O'Sullevan and his 50th and last commentary on the race, including the unveiling of his statue by the Princess Royal. They also covered the parade of past winners, and there were interviews with Ginger McCain, trainer of the incomparable Red Rum, Mick Fitzgerald – winner in 1996 on Rough Quest – and Gee Armytage.

'The rehearsal had gone well, and the whole of the build-up went extremely well,' said Martin. 'Everything was light-hearted and good. We showed the first race at 1.45 p.m., then Des had the "Mama Sans", as we called them. They were a group of 12 Singapore night club hostesses, brought over by the sponsors as a thank you for all their hard work during the year. We confronted Desmond with 12 of them, none of whom spoke English. Des was not too pleased with us.'

Mike Atherton, England's cricket captain and a part of the crowd, was also interviewed and the second race of the day was shown without hitch. Martin then recalls Desmond and Jenny Pitman, a double act on the big day which has run for years, doing their showpiece. 'It was an exceptional interview,' said the producer. 'She suggested it was about time Des made his live-in lady a respectable woman. Jenny was about to do the same with her fella, which she has since done.'

Desmond, although brushing off the trainer's remarks with a light-hearted comment, was not impressed.

'She invaded my private life in front of about 14 million people,' he said. 'I was talking to a friend the other day and he said my eyes suddenly went cold when she said that. I just thought at the time that if I invaded her private life on television like that she would not have liked it, and I didn't like it either. But we made a joke out of it and on we went. I thanked her for sharing it with the British public.'

Despite that uncomfortable moment, Des was pleased with the way the show was going. 'Some years it goes well and some years it doesn't,' he said. 'Some years people give you something in interviews and some years they don't; some years you ask good questions and some years you don't. I felt this year it was terrific, it seemed to have gone very well. I felt good, enthusiastic, interested, had fun. We even had Gregory Peck on. We had some very good interviews.'

The 2.55, the Martell Aintree Hurdle, was run seemingly without problems for the BBC crew and they started gearing up for the big event. Desmond was standing in the unsaddling enclosure where he would watch the race on a monitor so he could be in prime position when the winner returned; Julian Wilson and Jim McGrath and the others took up their locations, nerves began to twitch inside the two scanners.

'It started off with Peter O'Sullevan, who was in the jockeys' room so he could do a double check on their colours,' said Martin. 'Then we were switching between the paddock which Richard Pitman and Peter Scudamore were commentating over. The early horses were coming out and we'd just done the runners and riders sequence which is very complicated, going right through every single runner in the race. At that point it had all been running well, there hadn't been a blemish that I can recall.'

Desmond says: 'There was an underlying feeling about the security on the Friday night; it crossed our minds but we came to the simplistic conclusion that the IRA were never going to do anything where horses are concerned. We kind of ignored it when it happened and it was as huge a shock to us as everyone else.

'I was in my area, where the interviewer has always traditionally watched the race from a monitor. I have a couple of guys with me and we talk about it as the race is going on; one horse falls and I cross it off the list and so on.

'On my sheet I've got a little yarn about whichever horse wins. You're hoping for a story, a guy who bought the horse that morning or his wife bought it for him, whatever, and then you can deal with it. Then of course this thing blew up and I was told we couldn't broadcast from that position anymore. I heard the warnings and I said; "Oh god this is dreadful". Then I was told I had to move as well and then they said to me that they would give the commentary over to the others.'

The BBC at that point were broadcasting pictures from the Parade Ring, where Richard Pitman and Peter Scudamore were assessing the chances of the various horses. Richard was not to know the prophecy of his words as he said: 'There is a great history of things being thrown up in this race.' A few second later news of the evacuation reached him.

Malcolm, producing his first Grand National, said: 'It was all in full swing and I remember hearing over the whole public address system, out of the blue: *Operation Aintree, Operation Aintree*. I thought "shit, something's wrong".

'I vaguely remembered the warnings from when I was working at Euro 96. If you heard "Operation Euro 96" you knew there was a serious security problem. At Aintree, I thought it was initially alerting all the security staff. It wasn't for the public but it triggered us off. I thought this was going to get bigger before it got smaller. We kept on covering the horses and then the whole of the stand was gradually evacuated.'

Desmond interviewed Nigel Payne at the scene and after being told to move, handed over to his colleagues before encountering problems he had not expected. 'A senior policeman came over to me and Chris White, the floor manager, and said to follow them,' he recalls. 'So we followed him and we found we were in this extraordinary group of people including Gregory Peck.

'We were being taken out of the place and we had this broadcast to complete, we had a few more hours to do. I said to Chris: "We can't follow them, they're taking us out, they think we want to go". So we then had to push our way back in again against the throng of people going out. Then we were told to go back to where the broadcasting vans were which was through another maelstrom of people.

'People were saying: "Hey Des, what's going on?" They were asking me where I was going, shouldn't I be on the television, so I was having to field all this while trying to get back.' The commentary was switched to Jim McGrath perched on some scaffolding 30 feet up by Becher's. He only had pictures being fed to him, had no other form of information, and for the next 15 minutes produced a remarkable piece of television for the millions of people watching around the world.

'To be very honest, with only 20 seconds' notice, I had no chance of preparing for what was demanded of me from high up on my perch,' said Jim. 'In fact, I was preparing to leave when "stand-by Jim" came over my earphones.

'It was then that I realised that with every one of my fellow commentators evacuated I was to be holding the baton. Malcolm Kemp was feeding me different shots from various parts of the track where cameras had been locked into position by departing cameramen. I just described the scene as best I could. Malcolm fed me with whatever information he was able to gather and I just pressed on. I was lucky to have Gordon Brown of *The Racing Post* working with me, particularly as the day before he had written a feature on the Aintree security arrangements. This was a great help as he had some facts and figures I could use.

'I was very aware of the need not to surmise or speculate. In such a serious situation this could have been very dangerous. I have since been told that I spoke for 13 minutes and 50 seconds, which I find amazing as it seemed just like a couple of minutes. It was a very strange experience.'

Martin paid tribute to that remarkable piece of work when he said: 'Jim McGrath was the last person to commentate because everyone had forgotten him. Security didn't know he was out there. He did a brilliant job. The pictures were excellent and so was he and he should be saluted for that.'

Desmond, meanwhile, had managed to battle his way back to the BBC scanner where Howard Woosey had managed to rig up his camera. He was joined by Jamie Osborne, Richard Dunwoody, Norman Williamson, Chris Maude, who by now were beginning to realise the seriousness of the situation as the crowds thronged towards the middle of the course.

After another engineer rigged a DVC camera and fed it live through a video tape machine for a brief spell with Richard and Peter from inside a scanner, it was back to Des. 'He started off talking to Toby Balding,' said Martin. 'Then of course Jenny

Pitman, who was tearful and was cross with everyone. Then fortunately, because we were definitely running out of things to do, Charles Barnett came into view and conducted that marvellous statement where he ordered all of us to leave.

'Because we're *Grandstand* they were able to pick up in London and Gary Lineker, who was presenter of *Football Focus* and was staying on for *Match of the Day*, got called up at very short notice and suddenly found himself presenting *Grandstand* for the first time in his life.'

Gary remembers the ordeal well. He was in the production office of TC5 at Television Centre watching the football action in preparation for the evening's programme. In one corner of the room was the Aintree coverage. 'We didn't have any sound but it was quite obvious that something was going on when we saw floods of people leaving,' he said. 'We turned up the volume, but certainly at that stage I did not think I would be sitting in the presenter's chair. The message came through that they might have to abandon transmission from Aintree and I was told I might have to take over. I said I'd better put a tie on then.

'All of a sudden Des was out and within five or ten minutes I was sitting in the chair, having had very little experience presenting on television. Things like *Football Focus* are planned; I write the scripts and autocue and questions but this was obviously a different matter altogether, such a huge day and a huge audience and no time to prepare. It was one of the scarier moments of my life. Similar sort of thing to taking penalties for England except it lasted a lot longer. I was ad-libbing into the camera and with such a delicate situation we had to be careful. We sort of busked it through and got to half-time and then they showed some old film. I then had a 20-minute crash course in the vidiprinter which I didn't think was as hard as it is. Eventually, I ended up doing the most bizarre thing – interviewing Des from Aintree on the phone. It was sort of surreal really. Without my radio experience I would have been totally stuffed. I felt totally shattered but it was a hell of an adrenaline rush.'

Desmond, by now stood down for the day, recalls an interesting few hours in the jockeys' car park. 'It was strange, like it must have been in war time. Everyone became jolly. Instead of being really fed up and moaning they were wandering around, wondering what was really going on. We found ourselves in this big marquee and there were people in there dispensing drinks and sitting round and having a jolly good laugh. I joined them for a bit because I didn't know what to do. They said we would obviously not continue and no one knew at that stage whether there would be a Grand National or not that year. We had a bit of a party.'

He then managed to get his car out, despite police instructions not to allow any vehicles to leave. 'My day's work was finished and then I wanted to get out,' he said. 'The police chief gave me permission to get my car out and that upset a lot of other people, but he said I had a special reason for going.

'I had borrowed a Jaguar XK8 sports car from a company to do a bit of a write-up on it and it had to go back the following day to pass on to someone else. By then there were hints the race would be run on the Monday so there was no way I was going to go home. I stayed in Liverpool and Rosie, my partner, drove the car all the way back to London. She was quite terrified of this brand new very high-powered car, worth around £60,000, and which she had never driven.'

Martin had gone straight into meetings with Lord Daresbury, Charles Barnett and others, assuring them the BBC would cover the Grand National whenever it was decided to run it. In that group were also Judith Menier and Patrick Martell and Martin says: 'Patrick was there looking concerned. If any man has had a difficult association with the Grand National it has to be him because ever since he took it over there has been a story. But he has stuck with it very bravely, especially as he had no idea what National Hunt racing was all about until he joined up.

'I told them we would do the race whenever it happened. I told them not to worry about that. We could cover it Sunday morning, Sunday afternoon, we'd clear the network whatever happened. Then the logistics took over and it became clear it couldn't happen on the Sunday.

'I went back to the hotel and there was a bit of a wake. We had come for our race and it hadn't happened. The transmission had been going extraordinarily well and so it was all so disappointing.

Saturday evening was cold, miserable and we were well pissed off at being mucked around by a bunch of lunatics.'

Malcolm recalls: 'We were up until 5 a.m. on Sunday morning because everyone was so keyed up. You get right up there and suddenly it's whipped from under you. Nobody wanted to go to sleep. We just wanted to keep talking.'

There was, however, little time to look back over the traumatic events of Saturday. By the following mid-morning the BBC were aware the race was going to be staged the following day, and there was little time to prepare. Some of the last, sad shots from Saturday had shown a few mindless individuals jumping up and down on the Aintree fences as they were evacuated from the course. It was not just the groundsman this concerned; many of the 40 BBC cameras were actually stationed within the fences.

'There was a lot of concern,' says Martin. 'We wanted to make our side of things as good as possible but there was no way of checking the damage because we weren't allowed out on the course. In the end the police did escort BBC engineers around every site at the end of Sunday so we could check everything. Amazingly far less had gone wrong than people at first thought.'

Desmond's Sunday was slightly more relaxed. 'Liverpool were playing at home and I brought them no luck because they were beaten by Coventry and it ruined their championship chances. Also at the match were three or four of the jockeys, still wearing their riding breeches because they couldn't collect any of their gear. Although I was at Anfield my thoughts were with the other people; Charlie Barnett and the rest of the people at the course and the police. They were having a terrible time, terrible stress for them.'

The race day was probably even more tense for Malcolm. He recalls: 'The real nerve-racking bit came on Monday. It was my first Grand National, it is a massive event, there was a lot of expectation on the product and with anything like this you like a bit of a run into it. I was pretty uptight, I have to say. Suddenly you're on air, you're covering the horses in the parade ring and I was nervous, and there would be something wrong with me if I wasn't. Because of what happened on Saturday you've probably got a bigger viewing audience because a lot of people switch on to see what will happen. I was just over the moon that everyone pulled together; largely Aintree, the police and us, because we all wanted it to happen.'

Desmond says: 'It was a big success, fantastic success, We were amazed by the television audience of around 12 million people. It was a great atmosphere and when Peter O'Sullevan came on to do an interview the crowds were giving him huge cheers and singing. Despite that I had heard hints of the warnings and we were all a bit tense because we thought this could very well happen again.'

'Everyone was really up for it,' says Martin. 'There was a feeling that no matter how many telephone warnings were made, this race would be run. There were lots of different plans to cope, all of which we were kept informed of. That was a bit unusual because the police don't normally give away their detailed secrets to a broadcaster but we were part of the team which made the Grand National happen and make it happen each year, so they trusted us and hopefully we were useful to them.

'On Monday at 4 p.m. we went on air again. The crowds were pouring in and it was clear it was going to be a very successful transmission for us. They all came, a lot of them local people who had been involved over the weekend opening their doors to the other racegoers. It became clear our audience on television was likely to be good and indeed it was. It was such a bloody good race.

'I think it was typical of the Grand National. It's much, much bigger than a horse race. It's an event and it always has been and always will be. It always turns into something. It doesn't matter how prepared you are. And this applies to the race organisers, the horses and jockeys, the television crews. You know there are going to be some surprises. Something always happens.'

Desmond says: 'Looking back, I think the serenity of it all was what amazed me. If there were bombs here and there you would expect people to be fearful and panicking, but there was no panic. No one was rushing, no one was barging around. They kept their humour and I thought it was marvellous.

'It did spoil the day for everybody there and the millions of viewers as well, although in a strange sort of way it did make great television. There was an absolute drama unfolding before you. Normally it's a horse race; this wasn't a horse race, this was something different. In the same way that events a few years earlier heightened people's interest. That wasn't a disaster it was just a cock-up, but it was a dramatic cock-up and very well worth watching.

'I was more shocked in 1993 than by this. Bomb scares do happen nowadays. We are almost used to it, horrifyingly. But for that race not to start, and then start half-heartedly was so bizarre. I remember saying to someone that it was the biggest cock-up that had ever happened in sport, and that it was going to be an extraordinary story – and it was.'

'On this occasion I was downhearted. I was thinking what a waste of time, what point was being made, that it was just spoiling everyone's fun. It didn't change anyone's opinion and certainly didn't gain them any respect.'

Despite the drama, one Grand National will always stand out for Desmond. 'Every year there seems to be something different but the Aldaniti year in 1981 was the one that moved me so much because of Bob Champion's condition,' he said. 'Bob had been with us the previous year as our special guest on the radio. He had been going through his chemotherapy, he had no hair, he'd lost all his weight, you'd have given him a week to live, and he said he would love to come back and win the race. I thought: "You've got no chance, God bless you, God save you, but I wouldn't give you a hope in hell". To have been that close to him on that occasion and heard him speak like that was moving and I was so overjoyed for him the following year. It was so dramatic.'

10

The Press

OVER the years Aintree has received magnificent support from the press, although our relationships have not been without stressful moments. Part of our problem is that Aintree, being a course that holds so few meetings, is not able to provide permanent facilities in every department. However when you consider that 20 years ago Mike Dillon and I used to work out of a small caravan with telephone lines strung from the back of the County Stand offices, perhaps we have not done so badly to provide the level of facilities that we currently do.

At present we have a small press room, overlooking the parade ring which houses a maximum of 20 scribes. However, with more than 100 representatives of the press from all around the globe requiring accreditation to the meeting, we obviously need a far greater amount of space than that. We erect a huge marquee where we stage all our press interviews and provide telephone and computer sockets for a further 50 pressmen and women.

Aintree were the first racecourse to introduce Mark Popham's Racenews service, which is now recognised as a must at all major meetings. Mark provides a phenomenal service which includes the provision of full and comprehensive results of all races together with biographical details of winning connections. In addition the service sends a steady flow of news, stories and topical information to the media and is considered by many to be an essential part of a sporting event's press service.

Mark and I got the idea from the Breeders' Cup in the States and we believe that we have developed this to a far superior level. Mark put the concept to John Parrett, then Aintree Chief

Executive, and being the far-sighted guy that he was John decided to give the service a try. It is now used at Cheltenham, Ascot, Goodwood, Newmarket, Doncaster and other quality fixtures of this type. The real benefit of the service, if used properly, is that the racecourse has one control point for announcements. Everything that emanates from any level of the management is issued via Mark's service, at a time when the management has other critical decisions to make and functions to perform. Over recent years we have worked very closely with John Sexton and the Horserace Writers' Association to improve press facilities and it does seem to me that at last the press have realised that we are doing our very best under far from ideal circumstances.

I have always thought that the unattractive invasion of the winning connections by the press corps is something racecourses should try to eliminate. No one would wish to deny the press their stories but the much criticised huddles can sometimes be quite offensive to the eye and are often resented by owners, trainers and jockeys. We have gone a long way to solving this at Aintree by providing a headphone service around the outside of the enclosure whereby all the press can listen to the immediate BBC interviews and by staging a press conference after each race on the lines of other major international sporting events.

At Aintree we are lucky to welcome press from all over the world. As far east as Japan, China and Hong Kong right across the globe to California on America's West Coast. It gives us great pleasure when all these friends join us and sometimes I wish we could offer them more of the hospitality that we receive when we join them at their major meetings.

At the 1997 National we had as many visitors as I can remember and I really have no idea what they must have thought of what went on, or more importantly how on earth they handled the situation and how they reported the events when they returned home. The occasion was certainly well documented and from the many cuttings that we and our sponsors Martell have collated the reaction was one of initial sympathy and eventual praise.

Amazingly, quite a large number of our senior press representatives had only arrived at Aintree just in time for

Friday's card as they had stayed on in Dubai, host to flat racing's World Cup which had been re-scheduled to Thursday after monsoon-like rainstorms had forced Sunday's programme to be postponed. I wonder what odds Ladbrokes would have offered on this double? The Dubai World Cup and the Grand National both to be postponed in the most improbable circumstances and then re-staged in a matter of days. Maybe 10,000-1 would be somewhere close to the mark.

The build up period for press accreditation is always a chaotic period. I am not referring to our racing press but to some of the feature writers and news reporters, few of whom seem to realise when the Grand National is scheduled. It is staggering how many applications pour in during the last ten days and put enormous pressure on those responsible for handling the situation. It would be wonderful to say 'No' once in a while but that would be self defeating and you need the patience of Job to deal with all these demanding individuals who think you have nothing else to do but satisfy them. More experienced people than me tell me that this is how news journalists work, and it is something we have to accept. This may be so, but I think it is inconsiderate and I find it very difficult to accept that applications could not be made well in advance. Is that really asking too much for an event as big as the National? I'm sure events such as the Olympics and the World Cup would not be so accommodating.

On the Thursday of the meeting we traditionally hold a champagne reception to welcome the media to the three days. Charles Barnett and Patrick Martell say a few words and we present the winning tipster from the previous National meeting with an engraved armada dish and an engraved bottle of the exquisite Martell Cordon Rouge. Despite the absence of certain key men in Dubai we went ahead with the occasion although we had to hold over the top tipster presentation to Colin Mackenzie of the *Daily Mail* who, although he had not stayed in Dubai had been seriously held up on the M6 by the bomb activities.

All our press arrangements were working pretty well and John Sexton reported to me that the corps were quite happy. We were able to issue, for the second year running, record crowd figures and Tote betting turnover for both Thursday and Friday so we all entered Saturday in a bullish frame of mind. As I have said before, the first two days, whilst highly significant in terms of racing, are only the dress rehearsals as far as financial success to Aintree is concerned. This is somewhat different to the other great jump festival at Cheltenham whose crowds are much more level over their three days. Tote Gold Cup day is always the biggest crowd of the three but in nowhere near the same proportions as Aintree where Saturday's attendance is close to double the first two days added together. As the Aintree management continue to build on the three-day festival this differential is reducing fast and now our crowds on the first two days are significant. Not too many years ago I can recall figures of 5,000 to 6,000, now we are looking at crowds in the 20,000s.

Everything was ready for the final National build-up, and we had run through all the press conference arrangements with Racetech, who would be filming the event for the closed circuit operation and Mark Popham had selected his team of race spotters to move to our special Portakabin in the BBC compound where we identify the progress or otherwise of every horse. This is another example of the service we offer the media. Within ten minutes of the finish of the race we are able to publish to the world the undisputed result including where every horse finished, details of whether they fell, were brought down, refused, the times and distances. This is a scheme we developed with Martin Hopkins at *Grandstand* and all that it involves is monitoring all cameras on separate screens after the director has cut away for the benefit of the TV coverage. Our spotters are thereby able to concentrate on fences and sections of the course and note exactly what happens to each and every horse. Martin is able to use the information as a support to his slow motion replay which is such a popular aspect of the overall coverage and follows very soon after the race has finished.

Chris Poole had settled into an office in the main block equipped with telephone lines and his own TV ready to commentate for the BBC World Service and I visited the Winners' Enclosure to make some last minute adjustments to the photographers' presentation areas. It was also necessary to make sure our news crew camera used by Sky and ITN was correctly sited and that Ian Payne, Rob Hastie and the Radio 5 Live team were happy with their position.

At the time of the evacuation, after I had been interviewed by Desmond, I returned to Charles Barnett's office in the County Stand. As a consequence I had no idea at that time what was happening in our press rooms or indeed how Mark Popham was coping. In the latter regard I should have had no worries. Half of Mark's team were about to leave for their race analysis exercise in the BBC Portakabin and Mark decided to make a bee-line there anyway because he knew there were phone and fax facilities. The true professional that he is, Mark made sure that he had taken with him sufficient equipment so that wherever he was based he could at least operate and communicate. This foresight proved absolutely critical over the next few days.

After some while Mark, along with almost everyone else including Desmond and the BBC, was moved out of this area. Armed with all their gear, Mark's team set off for Joe McNally's house on the Melling Road. I was able to talk to Mark and Joe from this point on. By now Charles and I had moved over to the police control point where I was able to use one of the few available land lines. Using the mobile phones was impossible; reports suggested they had been barred for a period of time, which may have been because in certain situations they can trigger an explosive device.

In the police control point I was given the task of preparing statements to issue over the public address, although as it transpired very few people were able to hear anything, at least until the police helicopter came on the scene. At the same time I was able to forward the statements to Joe McNally and Mark was able to issue them as official bulletins to the national and local media. BBC Radio Merseyside really came into their own and acted as a catalyst for local news, which proved invaluable over the weekend.

Later on that evening when little more could be practically achieved, and a good night's rest would be the most valuable asset, Mark returned with his team to their accommodation and waited for instructions. After Charles, Peter Daresbury and I finally left the police station Peter decided that we should all regroup back at his house and decide our tactics. I seem to remember arriving at Peter's around 10 p.m., and his wife produced a welcome and delicious meal and we were able to enjoy some stimulating liquid refreshment.

We decided that there was a vital need to set up a temporary press facility and, with the Park Hotel only ten minutes from the course, that that would be the ideal choice. The other major advantage is that the Park is owned by the Greenalls Group so Peter was soon on the telephone and before too long the arrangements were made. Even though it was very late I called Joe and Mark and agreed with them that as early as possible on Sunday morning we would have the facility up and running and that we would endeavour to contact all the key press personnel and inform them that they could obtain information and use the facilities as they wished.

At Peter's house by then were Charles and I, David Hillyard, from Racecourse Holdings Trust, Ian Renton, John Sunnucks and Kevin Byram from Brunswick PR and an even later arrival was Andrew Tulloch who looked absolutely shattered. Peter rang the nearby Daresbury Park Hotel (another owned by the Greenalls Group) and David, John, Kevin and I decamped for some sleep whilst the others found a bed at Peter's. Peter's brother-in-law Johnny Weatherby was also staying and he and his Weatherby team were able to assist in the critical exercise of contacting trainers to see if they would run their horses in a Monday National. We agreed to reconvene at 8 a.m. sharp. The last thing and just about the only thing I could think of before I dropped off for the little sleep I was able to grab, was how all the racegoers and all my friends and colleagues were coping. At least I was lucky enough to have a warm bed to sleep in and was broadly able to keep in touch with what was going on.

After some breakfast the hotel party arrived back at Peter's house on the dot of eight and we were shortly joined by David Oldrey and John Smee from the British Horseracing Board, who were there to advise on all the technical issues involved in the running of the race. Basically unless we ran the Martell Grand National on Monday or at the very latest on Tuesday, we would open up a real can of worms because we would be entering the realms of needing to re-open the race, and all that that would entail. We now knew exactly what we had to do and it was fortunate indeed that we had the experts on hand to advise us.

By 9 a.m. Mark was setting up at the Park and we had decided that Kevin Byram with his vast media experience would join the press centre team. Mark has told me subsequently that Kevin was a real star and his input was immeasurable.

Peter, Charles, John and I set off again for our second home, Police HQ, where a mid-morning press briefing had been scheduled. Andrew Tulloch and Ian Renton had long since set off back to the racecourse. After a further meeting of Gold Command, which impressed me enormously, we set about preparing ourselves for the press conference. The progress throughout the night had been quite dramatic and the local authority, the social services and schools and community centres had all worked feverishly to do the best they could for the stranded racegoers.

Sunday morning's press conference was naturally enough much more crowded than Saturday evening's but as you would expect the general atmosphere was supportive and in no way hostile. Once again Assistant Chief Constable Paul Stephenson and Charles Barnett were the key players. The police chief was able to brief everybody on the activities in the city the previous night and to repeat much of the information that had been reported to him at the Gold meeting an hour or two earlier. Charles was able to update the press on the plans to repair the fences, to replace the running rails and to clear the debris from the track.

Charles was also able to advise that having contacted all trainers we had received overwhelming support and at best we would lose only one horse and at worst two. We had also made arrangements with Weatherbys that they should produce a full colour racecard for Monday and this would be free to all racegoers. Charles also confirmed that the BBC had agreed to cover the race in full at 5.00 p.m. the following day and would commit a minimum of two hours coverage to the event. Provided the police were totally satisfied that Aintree was clear of any explosive devices the race would be run. The police confirmed this and the stage was therefore set for the first ever Monday National.

Cars, it was stated, should be clear for pick-up later on Sunday and any vehicles not collected from the County or Central Car Parks that night would be removed to the Steeplechase Enclosure for collection at a later time. After several questions and one-to-one interviews we were clear to return to the racecourse and we arrived back, for the first time since late Saturday afternoon, at about 12.30 p.m.

The operation at the Park Hotel had been running smoothly and just about all the racing journalists were established there. Mark, Joe and Kevin had been joined by Lee Richardson, the Marketing Director of the British Horseracing Board, who was happy to do all he could to assist in the massive task of communications that was on hand. Mark had quite sensibly decided that Charles should meet the racing press head on at the Park and at 5.30 we arrived to answer their questions. They were enormously supportive and as Charles's voice occasionally broke through stress and emotion I could tell that anything he was able to tell them would be treated with the greatest deference. This was nothing like 1993 where the press would have been prepared to hang us out to dry; this was much more a case of pulling together and ensuring the show went on, no matter what. We left the Park after an hour or so and returned to the racecourse. Mark rang to say that the efforts Charles had made had been extremely well received and the whole press corps were 100 per cent behind the management.

During Sunday evening the phone was red hot with, amongst other things, requests for interviews with Charles on Monday morning. We decided that to be fair to Charles we would restrict these to a maximum of four, bearing in mind that he had the small matter of staging the National to think about. Any other interviews would be dealt with by Joe McNally or myself.

We met very early on Monday morning to plan our strategy and at about 8.00 a.m. we drove down to the front gates to complete the interviews. Silver Commander Ian Latimer was performing similar duties and both he and Charles were clear soon after 9.00 a.m. to return again to the main task in hand.

By about 11.00, the allotted time, the key members of the press turned up at the course not only to prepare themselves for the day ahead, but also to be reunited with all their belongings including their computers that they had been forced to abandon two days before.

Things never work out quite right and although we had told the press that 11 a.m. was the time, the police were still not satisfied that all was well. It was soon after 2.00 p.m. that we were able to allow access to the press rooms and only then if the press were prepared to confine their movements within that area. You do not have to be a genius to realise that if one area has been declared totally sterile you simply cannot allow free access until everywhere else on the course has been similarly cleared. At that time there were one or two areas well clear of the press rooms which had to be re-swept. Our press friends were very understanding, if somewhat bemused, and fortunately it was not too long before the police were totally satisfied that all was well and the whole site could be handed back to the course management and that when required the gates could be opened.

As far as the press were concerned everything then returned to a normal Grand National with Mark Popham back on site issuing updates on runners and trainers' comments as though nothing had happened. From my point of view we had the additional burden of how to handle the political press corps as John Major had decided fly in by helicopter to see the race accompanied by an enormous number of photographers and Downing Street press. This proved a real headache and thank goodness for Kevin Byram, who generously agreed to deal with this assisted by Lee Richardson. This kept them right out of my hair and I was and still am eternally grateful for this. Kevin has since told me that they were a real nightmare, some of the worst and most ill-mannered press he has dealt with and impossible to please.

One group arrived too late to be transferred to the grandstands and had to watch the race from the Steeplechase Enclosure. They were chaperoned by Lee Richardson, who has since explained that they were like lost souls out there busily trying to send back messages to their offices. Presumably they were telling their editors that they had arrived too late and that the Prime Minister was on the other side of the racetrack . . . Lee tells me that he was the only one who was cheering on the horses and riders as they raced towards the Melling Road and the home straight. I wonder if the political hacks knew what race they were watching?

For my part I had to accredit just about every news crew that exists. Although we expected an invasion we had not anticipated anything quite so large. News access is not an easy thing to deal with as there is nothing worse than a host of TV crews on site over whom you have little or no control. I was desperately concerned that none of the race was filmed, thereby putting us in breach of our BBC Sport contract. I knew that once on the course the crews would be uncontactable so I sought out Lord Daresbury who immediately suggested that we go and see the BBC to clear things with them. This we did and Martin Hopkins totally understood our position and told us that under these unique circumstances we could not possibly be expected to control these crews. 'They all know the rules,' he said. 'Don't worry about it.' We did insist that every crew sign an undertaking not to film any part of the race. These are all on file at Aintree.

The race was run and once again Aintree produced a magical result. Our post-race press conference, ably hosted by Geoff Lester, could have been Saturday's. The coverage the next day was the best ever.

* * * * *

Inspector Ray Galloway works in the press office of the Merseyside Police, based at Canning Place. He is part of the team, some officers, some civilian, dealing with the hundreds of daily inquiries about incidents in the region, calls from television and radio stations and local and national press. His interpretation of events will often be seen or heard by millions of members of the public, so it is a crucial role where he has to get the balance just right.

Inspector Galloway's task on Grand National day was to be stationed within the press room and adjoining marquee, handling questions about security, about incidents on the course and other matters which may have been raised. He would liaise with his senior commanders to protect them from thousands of questions.

Inspector Galloway, of course, did not expect to be carrying out the role which transpired; passing on the news to the journalists and the world that a major incident was happening, one which would have repercussions so far reaching no one could have imagined the consequence of his announcement.

He was standing within the press area and recalls: 'My abiding memory was when one of the special branch officers came up to me with his pager and held it in front of my face. I read it and it said: *Authenticated phonecall. Evacuate now.*

'Our eyes met and it was a look which told me I knew my role. He didn't say anything, just nodded his head and walked off. I went up on to the stage, gave the microphone a little tap and said: "Excuse me, ladies and gentlemen, we have had an authenticated phonecall and we need to evacuate."

'If I'm honest the reaction was "on yer bike". I then had to change my tone and said: "Ladies and gentlemen, this is serious. I'm absolutely serious. We need to evacuate these premises now. Everybody should follow me."'

The response was, to say the least, cynical. Gathered in the two areas were some of the most senior racing and sports journalists in the country. Their attitude to a bomb scare was to shrug their shoulders and let others worry about it. Newspapers had to come out, sports editors and editors had to be satisfied, and that could not be done without direct access to information. Let the police worry about the call, and when the fuss was all over they would put a line or two about it in their copy.

Malcolm Folley is chief sports reporter of the *Mail on Sunday* and was preparing himself for the National, ready to write around 1,200 words on the drama of the event. He was assisted by freelance journalist Laurie Brannan with the newspaper's racing editor, Ivor Herbert, watching the race from home. Ivor, one of the profession's more senior writers at the age of 72, believes he can get more information 200 miles away than being on the course.

As for those at the scene, Malcolm recalls: 'I was sitting upstairs in the old established press room. I was just getting my things together before the race when the announcement came. It was clear from his tone that this was not a dress rehearsal. I have heard lots of security announcements down the years at Wimbledon, and you know you will get the all-clear after about three minutes. But in this case with the urgency of the voice and the speed at which people were being asked to leave the building, I realised that we had a full scale emergency in progress. I was lucky in that I had all my stuff around me and I took the precaution of grabbing everything; my computer, my notes, my phone, the lot. I just made a lucky call and got it right.

'We're all cynical in the press and we've seen lots of things over the years. We were thinking we would be back in ten minutes or so which is why not everybody grabbed their things. I had no reason to think otherwise either but I just took it all with me.'

Howard Wright is assistant editor of the *Racing Post*, and the three days of the Grand National meeting do not come any bigger for the trade papers. This particular April he was given special access to the BBC, shadowing their top executives in order to write a feature on the way the channel covers the event. 'It is the biggest day of the year for the *Racing Post*,' he said. 'It is easily the biggest circulation day and the way that the meeting has been structured and improved over the last four or five years into a proper three-day festival means that it has become even more important.

'*Racing Post* circulation increases with TV coverage quite naturally and the way that the meeting's quality has improved almost out of recognition has added to the betting interest, the TV interest and along with it has driven circulation upwards. It has become a very big focal point, as big as Cheltenham and Royal Ascot and bigger in one sense because it builds up to the Saturday.

'It struck me it might be an interesting idea to follow what the BBC did at the meeting, how they covered the meeting from a production point of view, and I was fortunate to have tremendous access. Things were going in an orderly direction and I was very pleased with it; I was able to see how everybody was approaching the week from the preparation on the Wednesday, the first briefing meetings between Malcolm Kemp, Dave Gordon and Martin Hopkins, who were leading the various teams. Malcolm Kemp was very interesting because it was his first Grand

National for the BBC, he was slightly nervous but full of expectation and anticipation.

'It was illuminating to see the whole thing being brought together for the first transmissions on the Thursday. As we went through Thursday and Friday I saw more people at work, went out in the country with Jim McGrath to see how they tackled the operation down at Becher's, went in the scout car to see how the new bubble camera was operating, watched Martin Hopkins producing from the most amazing scanner that you could possibly see. Just generally gathering my thoughts to see how I would approach a feature written for the following week.

'That was still going in the way I anticipated it at Saturday lunchtime and I'd arranged that my last job would be to watch the Grand National itself from the scanner in which Malcolm Kemp was operating. Everything was proceeding quite normally and according to schedule. In the event I had a unique observation of the National because I could see it building up from all parts of the course.'

Howard's feature was soon to take on new dimensions: as he was sitting in the scanner the alert went off. 'I had an almost detached view of what was happening,' he said. 'It became obvious very quickly that this was a major incident. It was taking place right outside the scanner van but I could have been anywhere in the world. That was what made it so fascinating.'

While Howard felt cocooned, Malcolm Folley was more in the front line. 'We got outside the press rooms and there was a very subdued mood,' he said. 'We were on the concourse behind the main grandstand where there were thousands of people. Being used to football crowds you shuffle along and when we got to the first bar I will always remember that there were people unwilling to put their drinks down and a lot of alcohol had been taken, as you can imagine by that stage of the afternoon. They were refusing to leave the bars, and not being asked to leave, so they were causing bottlenecks as thousands of us were trying to go through this small area. There was the main gate of Aintree immediately to our left but we weren't allowed to go down there. That meant we had to join thousands of the punters and the hundreds of guys still unwilling to treat it seriously. It took us a good ten minutes to shuffle along to the gate they asked us to leave from. It was a one-way system but people were trying to go back in the opposite direction. There was just a sense of panic in the air for a while. That was probably the only time I felt uncomfortable.'

As soon as he reached the car park by the main gate, Malcolm found many of his press colleagues; James Lawton from the *Express*, Hugh McIlvanney of the *Sunday Times*, Roy Collins, David Barnes and others. 'I haven't ever evacuated a sporting event along with 60,000 people, so there was this feeling of confusion,' he said. 'We were standing in the car park and we all started to reach for our mobile phones and you couldn't get a call out. It took a few minutes for it to dawn that clearly the radio signals had either been purposely jammed or there was overcrowding.'

By now, the press journalists were beginning to worry about the time. Malcolm had managed a brief call to the office before being evacuated from the press room, but knew his sportsdesk and, indeed, the newsdesk would be desperate for information, although they probably knew more than he did with the benefit of television.

'We realised after about 15 minutes that we had a major story on our hands,' he said. 'It clicked that we were sitting on top of something that was both genuine and huge. If they had taken the trouble to take us all out like that they clearly believed there was a device or a bomb inside Aintree.

'We then got out on to the street and were trying to get to the main gate to work out some chain of communication with the police. We needed someone to tell us precisely what they were doing and what procedures had been put in place. Nobody from the police would talk to us; the highest rank we could find were constables and they seemed to be as much in the dark as us; sergeants were no better informed and eventually we found some guy with two pips on his shoulder and he either didn't know or was unwilling to talk to us.'

Howard was transfixed in the BBC scanner as the drama unfolded. 'The job had to be done,' he said. 'It had become the biggest event of the weekend and here were guys who were not used to covering news stories. It was a wonderful place to see everything happening. Almost a sort of voyeurism, seeing something happening which in effect you had no part of. The calm of the crowd was actually translated into the calm of the broadcast. Between the two there was this frenetic atmosphere of doing the job, of relaying what was happening to the rest of the world. It suddenly became obvious to me that the job I was doing for the *Racing Post* had also changed. I was seeing something very different, something that had never happened before. I almost had to tear up what I had done.

'It was an eerie feeling seeing Peter O'Sullevan, the man who should have been commenting on the climax to the greatest race in the world, having to stand in a scanner van watching the events that were crushing his big day. The way that the BBC team evacuated their positions one-by-one at the latest possible moment was symptomatic of what was happening all round the course.

'Then Charles Barnett was being interviewed by Desmond Lynam. In one sentence he summed up the whole dramatic trauma of the day, saying *Everyone Must Leave*. Here was a guy telling even the BBC what to do.

'Charles was the man who turned the BBC broadcast because at that point Martin Hopkins picked up exactly what was being said to Desmond and used the line: "No more talking, take over in London". That was when Gary Lineker, looking like a frightened rabbit, had to take over in a role that was entirely alien to him. He had to suddenly take over the biggest news story of the entire weekend. That was the point that Martin Hopkins and his team left their scanner, and I left my post. From being detached from the event I became part of it, part of the crowd. I made one brave attempt at professionalism, following Dave Gordon and Martin Hopkins to the police control point and was firmly and politely told there was no entry.

'Having started off doing an insight into how the BBC were covering their biggest sporting outside broadcast of the year it had all changed completely. It was an enormous bit of luck to be in the right place at the right time. It was one of the best jobs I have done and a bold step for the BBC to allow someone in there.'

The pressure on Malcolm Folley and his colleagues, meanwhile, was becoming more intense. The deadline for first editions of Sunday newspapers is around 6 p.m., and they still had not managed to make contact with London. 'We knew the offices would know what was going on because they had the television screens. We also knew they would be frantically trying to contact us,' he said.

'At that point, instinctively, we all drifted away. I discovered about half an hour later that everyone had done the same as me; gone and knocked on the door of one of the houses nearby and asked to use the telephone. I went to a house a few doors down from the main entrance and there was a radio reporter already using the phone in there. The house owner very kindly said I could come in and when the other guy had come off the phone I spoke to the sportsdesk and then was put through to the newsdesk because the story was becoming much bigger than merely for the back pages.

'I was immediately asked to write 900 words for the front of the newspaper and at that point I had absolutely no idea what was happening at Aintree. We were living completely on rumour and speculation. There was no way of knowing anything official. All you could do was describe the scene that we had been a part of.

'I started ad-libbing the piece and I must have been going for about 20 minutes and the radio guy came back in to use the phone. The householder virtually demanded I stop there, get off the phone and let the other guy use it. I said it doesn't work like that; we all have our jobs to do. The householder started getting very aggressive about the fact I should come off the phone so I had a word with the radio reporter and said: "Look, let me just finish a couple more paragraphs. How long will you be?"

'He said he was just going to do a minute live so that was fine; I could then finish off my piece. By now the householder was getting a little bit edgy about us tying his phone up so I left him and walked back over to get some more information back out in the street. We all congregated and there was a good camaraderie even though nobody knew anything. We were still operating, metaphorically and quite literally, in the dark.

'I went back 15 minutes later to use the phone again and the guy was not quite so hospitable this time. There was a sign in his window by now saying that he was selling beers. People were filing into his house off the streets and while I was on the phone I could hear voices raised in the front room and suddenly the doors being blocked and there was a scuffle. The householder was saying: "You're not going anywhere" and someone else was saying: "This is his house".

'It became very, very close to a full-scale fight breaking out. Two guys had come in and there had been an exchange of insults, either perceived or real, and the house owner and his brother-in-law were mightily angry and in the time-honoured Liverpool way were going to sort it out.

'I was on the phone and I was having to back against the stairs and get out of the way as they are pinning people against the wall. My safe house had become a very unsafe house and I thanked him very much for the phone and disappeared just as they were heading out into the street to sort it out.

'I discovered from Jim Lawton that he had a much safer safe house a few doors down and he agreed very kindly to let me share it. He extended the same invitation to Hugh McIlvanney and all three of us were in there and being brought cups of tea by the owners. It was lovely. We must have used their house for the next hour and a half.'

Despite the calmer location, Malcolm knew the back pages of the *Mail on Sunday* needed filling with a sports angle to the great evacuation. Early editions had been cobbled together, with the front part of the newspaper carrying all the official information which had trickled out of Aintree. Malcolm decided to try and track down Richard Dunwoody, the twice Grand National-winning jockey and a friend. 'We didn't know where the jockeys were but we knew they would have been evacuated from the premises along with everyone else. News was also beginning to filter through about the stable lads looking after the horses but we couldn't confirm any of this because we had no way of checking it out; we were only 400 yards away from where it was all happening but we may as well have been on another planet.

'We walked up and down outside Aintree looking for the

jockeys but by now the atmosphere in the streets and the pubs was getting uglier; there were people who should have known better screaming at the police and attendants to have the right to go in and get their cars. They were getting really, really nasty with polished vowels and ugly language.

'I managed to speak to Laurie Brannan and he had phoned a hotel in Runcorn where lots of the Grand National fraternity stay and got two rooms for us that night. He also established that Richard might be among the jockeys who were staying there.

'It was well after 8 p.m. by now and our next problem was to get to the hotel because all our cars were locked within Aintree. We tried to get a taxi to take us to Runcorn but failed. The people in the house which I was in must have tried four or five taxi companies and we were being told there were four-hour delays because every taxi in Liverpool was out working. We asked the householders for one more favour: would they mind driving us to Runcorn, obviously offering to pay the petrol money. The guy agreed and we headed off there, dropping Jim Lawton off in the town and going to the hotel.

'As Laurie was checking in I grabbed the house phone and was put through to Richard's room. We arranged to meet and he turned up, still in his riding boots, also with his girlfriend Emma. We sat down and I was furiously taking notes as Richard told me the amazing story of how he escaped in the back of a horsebox. A photographer came in and took a snap of them both and I managed to file the story for the sports pages by about 10.20 p.m.'

His work done for the evening, and satisfied that the *Mail on Sunday* had an exclusive story on the sports pages, Malcolm joined Richard, Emma and several other members of the racing fraternity for a meal and a few glasses of wine and they discussed the traumatic afternoon.

'The atmosphere by then was one of defiance,' he said. 'We all realised that extreme precautions had to be taken. Everyone connected with the race was saying that they could not let it be stopped, they would have to run, be it tomorrow, Monday or the next Saturday. Nobody had any self interest, nobody said it was too dangerous. Everyone was in it together.'

11

Sir Peter O'Sullevan

THERE are some people you come across in your life who fill you with awe. For any lover of racing one such man is Peter O'Sullevan, whose voice has been synonymous with the turf for longer than most of us can remember.

I've been lucky enough to know Peter for some 20 years, mainly because of my involvement in the National. During that time I have come to respect and admire him for everything he stands for, which I would sum up as pure class. Peter always has time for people and is a good listener and never ever makes you feel that you are wasting his time.

The 1997 Martell National was one to cherish and remember even before the events on Saturday. Not only was it the 150th running of the race but it was also Peter's 50th commentary. Just dwell on that statistic; one voice to call one third of all the Grand Nationals. During our discussions and planning for the promotion of the race meeting these celebrations always featured prominently and very often it was difficult for us to decide which was the more significant. Fortunately the two were so intertwined that it became easy to plan complementary activities.

The BBC had planned their own tributes to the great man and the media were all clamouring for interviews and a chance to record this most momentous of milestones. For our part we were very much beholden to the generosity of the Duke of Devonshire, who had commissioned a bronze which would overlook the famous Aintree paddock as a lasting tribute to the Voice of Racing. Her Royal Highness The Princess Royal had graciously consented to perform the unveiling ceremony at 1.20 on Saturday. Peter, being the great professional that he is, was frequently on the phone to me in the weeks prior to his big day to run through the arrangements and to ensure that the timings were spot on. He asked me to speak to *Grandstand* editor Dave Gordon, to make arrangements for a colleague to read the runners and riders for the first race in case he had not the time to return to his perch high in the County Stand after the formalities.

Peter was down and raring to go soon after 1.00. He was absolutely determined to be in the right place when the Princess Royal arrived. Also at his request I had organised a police officer to be with him all day so that he could move freely without too many time-consuming interruptions.

Peter and I waited anxiously beside the veiled bust, both of us thinking that the crowd was rather too close for comfort with a royal about to arrive. The police seemed to agree and with little fuss the enthusiastic well-wishers moved back several paces. The crowd didn't seem to bother the Princess at all and after a few well chosen words from Peter Daresbury, Aintree's Chairman, the deed was done, the veil removed, and there was Peter in all his glory for everyone to admire. We now have two statues at Aintree: one of the magnificent Red Rum, the other Peter O'Sullevan. What a grand double.

After the bomb alerts I lost contact with Peter and I have since discovered that he was desperately reluctant to leave the course on Saturday without all his treasured possessions: his briefcase, his notes, his fabulous charts and famous binoculars. There were however to be no exceptions and leave without them he did.

During the calamitous next few hours communications were virtually impossible, mobile phone lines were jammed and before too long my battery was totally flat, although the phone was still capable of taking messages. I always pride myself on returning messages but here was one occasion when this was impossible. When, many hours later I was able to listen to my scores of calls, several were from Peter desperate for news of his belongings, which he was convinced he would never see again. I felt really bad about not having been able to return these cries for help from such a man. I felt totally useless, I seemed to have let him down badly.

The next time I saw Peter was at dusk on Sunday. He appeared at our HQ on the course looking dazed and perplexed. When I caught his eye I could tell he was not best pleased that I had not been in touch but on hearing the circumstances he readily accepted that there was nothing I could have done. But here was Peter O'Sullevan and I knew we simply had to help him. I introduced him to the Chief Inspector in charge and after a short exchange it was agreed that Richard Thomas be allowed to be escorted to the top of the County Stand. I remember Richard and Peter disappearing into the twilight with an escort. I am delighted to say that Peter recovered everything.

*   *   *   *   *

The Grand National's transition to become an event without Peter O'Sullevan will not be easy; the doyen of racing commentators adds something special to the event which can never be replaced. No one would even attempt to supersede the man who first called in the horses for radio in 1947. That National, as with the majority since, produced a story which spread beyond the confines of the racing world. The weather that year had been devastating, bringing racing to a total stop until 15 March, barely a fortnight before the date of the big event.

There were 57 runners that day, the second largest field in history, Aintree was shrouded in mist and heavy rain, and the going could only be described as dreadful. Peter recalls Caughoo, one of the many 100-1 outsiders, smoothly cruising through the field to win by 20 lengths from Lough Conn. It was a marvellous triumph by Caughoo's jockey Eddie Dempsey, an Irishman who had not only never ridden at Aintree, but had never set foot in England until two days before the race.

Caughoo, an eight-year-old gelding bred from a pairing of the stallion Within-the-Law and the mare Silverdale, did not possess an ounce of jumping blood. That made it even more remarkable that the winner looked fresh enough to go round the formidable Aintree circuit again. Rumours soon started that, indeed, he had been round only once, and that he had taken refuge on the other side of the course, hidden by the mist, and resumed racing when the rest of the field approached for the second time.

Peter laughs when he recalls the story, insisting there is no way it could have happened. 'Eddie Dempsey compounded the rumours,' he said. 'He had hit skid row and was trying to get a few quid from some distinguished journal like *The People*. He allowed it to be inferred from them that he'd been extremely clever and hidden behind a haystack. Anybody who could find a haystack at Aintree deserved to get away with it!'

Born on 3 March 1918, Peter's is a career packed with memories, many of them coming from the Grand National. But he does not like to compare the years, rather allowing each new chapter to take its place in the richness of nostalgia. 'I think the comparison business is very invidious,' he says. 'How do you compare the drama, the emotion, of Aldaniti's triumph and Red Rum's third success? They are both different emotions and different responses and in their own way they are both very, very exceptional. The National is always a wonderful story, always dramatic.'

For this reason, he was not approaching the 1997 race in any unusual way, despite it being his 50th commentary, the 150th race and the fact he was being honoured by a royal presence to mark his contribution to the world's greatest steeplechase. 'To be absolutely honest it wasn't anything I was thinking about,' he said. 'When the trouble started I was never thinking "Oh what a shame that I'm not going to do my 50th". In the interviews of course I was saying I would be very happy to do it if we do restaged it, but I said I couldn't see that happening.

'Obviously the day had already become extra special for me because of the presentation. Because of that and my very tight schedule there was a very nice police officer looking after me. I had headed off to the weighing room, something I do before every National. When the last of the jockeys went through I said: "Right, we've got to move quickly now and get back up to the commentary position."

'The police officer said: "Hang on a moment."

'"What's the hold up?"

'"I'm afraid you're not going back up. We've been told to clear the course and I'm getting instructions now."

'"That's ridiculous. I must get back to the commentary point because if people have been told to clear the course I want to be up there and describe the scene."

'"There's no way I can let you up there."

'Earlier in the day Brough Scott had asked me if it would be okay to stand unobserved in the box while I did my last National. He said he would be totally unobtrusive and in the shadows, and of course I agreed.

'Brough was on my heels through all this and I said to the policeman: "This is ridiculous" and I was walking towards the steps with him following me, remonstrating quietly with Brough, as you do.

'I got to the foot of the steps and of course people were pouring down so it wouldn't have been easy to get back up but I said, "I must go back up. I want to see and to describe what is going on and furthermore I've got my phone up there, I've got my binoculars – they are the Beeb's, 10x80s mounted on a tripod. I've used them for centuries – my flat keys. I've got everything that I don't want to lose up there."

'He said: "There is absolutely no way I can permit this."

'"That's quite ridiculous. It is quite obvious it is a hoax anyway, an over-reaction."'

Peter turned to Brough, objecting again, when his colleague pointed out that the police were taking the whole incident very seriously, the stands were being cleared and they were taking every precaution.

'Right,' said Peter. 'I bet you £100 it's a hoax.' And the bet stood.

Peter adds: 'I kept remonstrating with my man but he said there is absolutely no way. He told me he had to follow orders and there was no way he would let me up into the stand.

'I thought back to 1974 when there was a similar incident at The Curragh on Irish Derby Day. There was a phone call, which the IRA inspired. The stands were cleared and there were only two people left, Michael O'Hehir and myself. Before it was cleared Ted Walsh and a few of them were up there and I offered them 1000/30 against them being blown up and Ted very nearly took it!

'We were up there on our own and I remember it because Michael was commentating to domestic viewers and I wasn't actually linked up with the Beeb at that time but waiting to get connected. I'd seen the Northumberland Plate on a two-inch screen black and white, very hazy, won by my horse Attivo. Then I received the message down the line there had been an objection. I turned to Michael and said: "There's a nice bloody thing. I'm going to get blown up before I know whether I've won the Northumberland Plate or not!" The objection wasn't to him in the end, it was the third to the second, so he won all right.'

That phone call in Ireland did turn out to be a hoax, and before long the crowds were allowed to return and racing resumed.

Peter says: 'My immediate thought at Aintree was that it was another hoax, but it sounded very clever. I offered 5/2 against the race being staged on Monday and evens against it being staged again that year, and there were takers. I couldn't believe it possible.

'I think it was enormous credit to the organisers that they were able to mend the fences, restage it as they did. Particularly to Charles Barnett because he was so steadfast throughout the entire occasion.

'We were unable to leave the course in our cars and Desmond Lynam was about the shrewdest because he managed to get his car and get out of the gates. Otherwise we were incarcerated, I felt for a rather needlessly long while.

'I was staying at the Moat House, situated in what someone humorously named Paradise Street. I was lucky to get back in because I had checked out that morning.

'The Sunday was total chaos because we were asked to gather at various control points in order to be taken to our cars and one thing and another. Nobody at the control points seemed to know what was happening. I spent the whole of Sunday trying to get my car out, just like everyone else, but what was more important to me was trying to get up to the commentary point. Eventually, I badgered the poor Chief Inspector Sue Wolfenden and I bet her £50 that by the time my belongings were recovered half of them would be missing.

'She said: "Absolutely nothing will be missing. We have the tightest possible security."

'You can't secure things,' replied Peter. 'There are some very special light-fingered characters around. There is no way you can inhibit their normal activities.'

Chief Inspector Wolfenden's promises were not enough to reassure the worried commentator, and he continued his campaign to be allowed into an area as yet unsearched by the police teams with their electronic equipment and their dogs.

'I finally got permission with my stalwart police shadow, who had linked up with me again,' said Peter. 'We got clearance and some idiot BBC studio manager intervened when we were on route to get back to the roof. And so we were frustrated.'

Despite the setback, he rallied again. 'Finally some time in the early evening Sue Wolfenden had Richard Thomas from Haydock escorted to collect my bag. When Richard returned I was relieved to see that the flat keys were there, the phone was there, my Jockey Club car park label was there, my binoculars were there, my commentary spectacles were there and my colour chart. I went up to the control point to press £50 into the hand of Sue Wolfenden. She backed away, the first time I had seen a Chief Inspector blush. She backed away towards her colleagues, who were all covered in scrambled eggs and gold buttons and things, and she held up her hands in horror and said there was no way she could accept it.

'I said: "Well you have to. I bet you 50 quid. That's it." A few days later I got an acknowledgement from the police orphanage fund thanking me for my contribution for the sum of £50.

'When it came to the Monday I couldn't believe the atmosphere could be generated and rekindled on the first day of the week like that. I remember Jim McGrath came to me and said: "You've had plenty of time to learn the colours, Pete."

'"Yer, and plenty of time to forget them, too."'

'It was a great tribute to the executive at Aintree. I thought they made a mistake when they let people in free because people don't appreciate what they don't have to pay for, but once again they were right.'

Peter was moved by a spontaneous rendition of *For He's a Jolly Good Fellow* by the Monday crowds and he added: 'I couldn't have been more wrong about the prospect of restaging it. I was so delighted that they did of course and so thrilled by the atmosphere; it was just the same in the weighing room, among the jocks, it was just the determination of everybody not to be frustrated, not to have one of England's premier sporting events, if not the premier event, ruined like that by some vicious idiot. It was tremendous.

'As for work it was like commentating on any other National. On a personal level I was annoyed with myself because at the weights conference we were interviewed and I had gone for Lord Gyllene. I had told anybody who asked me that this was the horse I could see going well, that he was a good jumper and seemed to enjoy it and then I persuaded myself to go along with J.P. McManus's horse Wylde Hyde.

'I started to switch allegiance and I hadn't had a bet by that stage and I went in on Wylde Hyde in the end. It wasn't the cash involved; I was just so annoyed at having been right initially and then changing allegiance. Otherwise it was a lovely race to cover except in the sadness of the two fatalities. A really exhilarating triumph by the winner and he could go on to win another.'

Peter fondly recalls the part played by the Princess Royal, such an admirer of his she had watched from his commentary box as he called the Martell Red Rum Steeple Chase on the Saturday. 'She was absolutely charming on the Monday because she said: "I'm so glad this has happened for you."

'My overriding memory was I suppose one of amazement that the race could be restructured and the atmosphere recaptured, that the charismatic ambience of the Saturday could actually be transferred to a Monday. I thought that was quite amazing. It was notable what a cheerful crowd they were.'

Peter carried on commentating until November 1997, and after his lifetime in the sport he is happy many of the traditions he first encountered have continued unaltered. 'There is so much less triumphalism in racing than many sports,' he says. 'It doesn't seem to generate the aggression that football does. Cricket is disappointing because it has become an almost violent spectator sport with shouting and swearing. The cricketers, like the footballers, don't behave as well as the horses. I mean the horses don't dash up and kiss each other and click hooves and do ridiculous things after a race. I'm all for the rider accepting success with grace and deference because it isn't him that has done it, it is the horse.

'I wouldn't want to inhibit the Frankie Dettori style because it's his special logo and it has been immensely successful and has widened the appeal of racing, but I think it would be an awful pity if it was widely copied.'

He now looks forward to continued enjoyment of the sport. 'I think I shall have all the excitement without the anguish,' he said. 'And I think if Aintree are kind enough to invite me I'm sure I will go to the Grand National. It's a great event.'

An immensely modest and charming man, Peter O'Sullevan's contribution to racing and particularly the Grand National will never be forgotten. An illustration of just how highly he is regarded came when his own colour chart for the 1997 race was bought at auction for £35,000 by J.P. McManus. 'I'd said to JP if it doesn't look like fetching £500 can you keep the bidding moving,' laughs Peter.

As Hugh McIlvanney, one of sports journalism's most astute observers once wrote: 'Peter O'Sullevan is widely accepted as the best horse-racing commentator in the history of broadcasting and possibly the most accomplished reader of action operating on any sport in the English-speaking world. His admirers are convinced that had he been on the rails at Balaclava he would have kept pace with the Charge of the Light Brigade, listing the fallers in precise order and describing the riders' injuries before they hit the ground.'

A fitting tribute to the man whose 50th and last Grand National commentary, thankfully, could not be halted by terrorists.